COOKING FOR YOUR FREEZER

COOKING FOR YOUR FREEZER

Mary Berry

octopus

Contents

This edition first published in 1979 by
Octopus Books Limited
59 Grosvenor Street
London W1

© 1977 Hennerwood Publications Limited

ISBN 0 7064 1130 7

Produced by Mandarin Publishers Limited
22A Westlands Road, Quarry Bay
Hong Kong

Printed in Hong Kong

Introduction

In an age which has produced all manner of labor-saving devices, the freezer is an excellent addition to household equipment. Not only is it an extra food store, but also an aid to menu planning, a stand-by in emergencies and a money-saver. But it must, of course, be used properly.

Cooking for the freezer is just as important as buying for it. The casseroles, pies, home-made soups and sauces, the cakes, pastries, toddlers' dishes which can be kept in the freezer make it a remarkable asset in the kitchen. Preparing double the quantities—half for now and half for the freezer—ensures having meals for emergencies and saves time when you are busy.

It will help the household budget too, for doubling the quantity does not mean doubling the cooking time. The amount of energy required to cook, say, one stew is the same as for cooking two.

Another advantage of the freezer is being able to cook when it is convenient and time is available. How many people throw away chicken carcasses, for example, simply because there is not time to turn them into stock. They can however be wrapped and stored in the freezer until time is available to turn them into stock.

Packaging for the freezer

Packaging is more than just a means of keeping the contents of the freezer tidy and separate. It helps to preserve the quality of the food, prevents dehydration and loss of nutritional value, stops strongly flavored foods from affecting others and inhibits bacteriological contamination between different items. For all these reasons, therefore, it pays to study the various methods of packaging carefully, decide which suits you best and buy accordingly.
Bags Plastic bags are exceptionally useful, capable of moulding themselves around awkward shapes and holding liquid if required. They come in various sizes, some with gussets and some without, separated, on a roll, colored and plain, and which you choose depends on the size of your family and how they will be used. Do buy the bags which are specially made for the freezer. They are thick enough to withstand the low temperature without splitting and if carefully washed and dried can be used again and again as a second wrap, but do not allow to contact food. Do not use bags supplied with clothes. Apart from the fact that they are not hygienic, they are also too thin to be satisfactory. *Boil-in-bags* are tough bags made to withstand being plunged straight from the freezer into boiling water. This makes them particularly valuable if you have to

go away leaving meals, mainly meat and fish in sauces, for those members of the family left at home. The dish can be prepared frozen, sealed in the bag, then heated without mess or bother. They are similar to the ones you buy containing cooked frozen meals. Other types of bag are made from aluminium foil, foil lined with plastic and paper lined with foil, and are bought with a strip seal.

Foil tins come in a great variety of shapes. Some have their own lids; others must be covered with foil. Their neat shapes make them particularly good for stacking. They are useful for complete meals, casseroles, pies and flans.

Rigid containers are usually supplied with lids and are ideal for liquids. The best are made of plastic and can be used in the refrigerator as well as in the freezer. Their tops should fit well and make an effective seal. Buy them specially for the freezer, making certain they are suitable for use at low temperatures, otherwise the plastic can become brittle and will not last long. Waxed cartons are effective and if handled carefully can be re-used if relined with a plastic bag. However they are not suitable for hot liquids and food should be cooled before being packed in these containers.

Freezer-wrap is an alternative to foil. It must be secured by means of adhesive *freezer tape*. Ordinary adhesive tape will not seal in low temperatures.

Improvised containers Don't throw away old yogurt or margarine cartons, particularly if you have a baby or toddler to feed. Enough puréed vegetables, stewed fruits, etc., for one meal, fit very nicely into a small thoroughly washed carton if it is relined with a new plastic bag. Do not use cracked containers.

Twist-ties and other seals Twist-ties, usually made from paper covered wire, are supplied with plastic bags. If you like gadgets, you can get twist-tie dispensers in which the wire comes in a continuous reel and from which you cut off the amount you need. Alternatively, there are special machines for sealing bags with adhesive freezer tape—home versions of those used by butchers. Keen freezer cooks can buy electric bag sealers but they are quite expensive.

Organizing the freezer

To be really efficient and economical, the contents of the freezer must be properly organized, so that you know where everything is and the items are used in strict rotation.

One of the best methods of storage involves grouping the same types of food together and always storing them in the same part of the freezer.

For really efficient storage it is possible to buy special stacking baskets which can be placed on the shelves of an upright freezer or stacked in the base of a chest freezer. Most chest freezers have room for three layers of baskets which helps to keep food organized in sections. Most chest freezers have one or more hanging baskets included in the purchase price. These can contain smaller articles, keeping like with like. Other baskets, some shallow, some deep, stacking or hanging, are available and enable you to make use of all the space in the freezer.

Color-Coding While not essential, this is a sensible aid to freezer planning. By giving a different color to each category of food and packing each item in an appropriately colored bag or using colored ties and labels, you can see at a glance where the meat or vegetables, the fish, fruit or pastries are.

Keeping a record Always keep a list of everything the freezer contains. This prevents items from remaining in the freezer for too long and enables you to plan a menu without removing the complete contents of the freezer to see what is available. It is possible to buy special record books with ruled columns for the item, date, quantity, etc. or you can use an exercise book and rule the columns yourself. Either way, see that it is kept near the freezer, together with a pencil or pen, so that entries can be made at once, or items crossed off as food is used.

Package shapes The freezer will run more cheaply and efficiently the less free space there is between packages and if it is kept well stocked. Obviously some things like roasts are bound to be awkwardly shaped, but if possible try to freeze items into cubes or "brickets". Liquids, for example, can be poured into a plastic bag fitted inside an old sugar carton or square plastic box. When frozen, the carton "mold" can be removed. A casserole dish may be lined with foil and filled with stew to freeze. When frozen remove the dish and return it to the kitchen. Before heating, the stew can be thawed and reheated in the same dish.

Freezing food

Quality, speed and hygiene are the three watchwords of really successful freezer cooking.

Freezing won't make food *better* than it is when purchased so you should always use the best quality ingredients—young vegetables, fresh meat and fish—for best results. Speed—in cooling before freezing—limits the build up of harmful bacteria and prevents ice crystals from forming in the food, and spoiling its texture. Freezing in small quantities ensures rapid, even freezing. Hygiene is always important in the preparation of food, and food being cooked for the freezer is no exception. Very low temperatures do not destroy bacteria, they merely make them dormant and food that is contaminated before freezing will still be contaminated when thawed.

Packing food for the freezer Some dishes, such as casseroles, can be frozen in a shallow meat tin. When firm but not quite solid remove from tin, dipping the base quickly into hot water if necessary to free the contents, then cut. Wrap each block separately, seal and label and return to the freezer. Remove as much air from the package, smoothing it out with the fingers before sealing. Where possible use shallow containers rather than deep ones, so that the freezing process is quick and even.

Sealing and labeling An airtight seal is essential. Give the neck of a plastic bag a couple of twists before securing with a twist-tie or freezer tape. Labeling is equally important. Stick-on labels may be used, especially on foil, or you can write directly onto plastic bags with a permanent felt-tipped marker. Make certain the bag is dry.

The label should give as much information as possible since the contents of transparent packages look different when frozen. The quantity should be given—either by weight or the number of people it will feed. The date on which the food is frozen, or the date by which it must be used, should be shown. The dating method should be consistent and the family should be made familiar with it.

Fast freezing Most freezers, unless they are very

small, have a fast-freezing switch, which is manually operated. This over-rides the thermostat and allows the temperature within to drop below the normal running temperature of 0°F, reaching −18° to −22°F. The lower the temperature the faster the food will freeze. The temperature drops throughout the whole cabinet but the coldest places will be near the sides where the freezing elements are situated. Chest freezers usually have a fast-freeze compartment with freezing elements in the dividing wall, and it is wise to keep this free from general storage. In upright freezers, the top or bottom shelf should be used, unless your model has a special fast-freeze shelf. The reason for having special compartments is to keep the un-frozen packs away from the remainder of the contents. Even when cooled, the newly prepared food will have the effect of raising the temperature of the items with which it comes into contact and even, temporarily, of the air within the fast-freeze compartment. This is why you should not try to freeze too much at any one time—the maximum amount is 10 per cent of the freezer's loading capacity in 24 hours. Remember to operate the fast-freeze switch before you plan to do any freezing as it takes two to three hours for the temperature to be reduced. It must be left on until the food is frozen all the way through, allowing about 2 hours for each pound of meat, poultry, fish, pies and cooked meals, or

1 hour for each pound of vegetables, fruit, liquids, cakes and bread. This is very approximate: naturally a deep thick parcel takes longer to freeze than a shallow thin one.

Open freezing This is a method of freezing food before it is packed. It is particularly convenient for food which would be a nuisance if frozen firmly together, such as vegetables, cakes, rissoles, fish cakes, etc. It is essential to open freeze items which squash easily, such as the decoration on iced cakes. Open freezing may be used to make storage easier. Garden peas, for example, can be divided into the amounts needed for a meal, packed in bags and frozen. With open freezing, however, the peas will be separated and, once frozen, will flow freely and can be packed into one bag and used in small quantities when needed. For open freezing, the items are spread on a special stacking open-freeze tray or onto a baking sheet lined with foil. They are packed into containers only when frozen solid.

Freezing vegetables

Only freeze vegetables which are young and freshly picked. Start by preparing them as if for immediate use. Always wash well.

All vegetables are better if they are blanched before freezing; that is, scalded briefly in boiling water. A blanching basket is usually recommended for the purpose, but a nylon muslin wine-straining bag bought from a home brewing shop is just as effective. Using only a small quantity at a time, put the prepared vegetables into the bag or basket and lower into boiling water. Take the blanching time from the moment the water comes back to the boil. Each

batch must be cooled before being packed into bags, sealed and labeled, and placed in the fast-freeze compartment for freezing. Cooling is carried out by immersing bag or basket in cold water to which you keep adding ice cubes. Alternatively, the vegetables can be put in a colander and cooled under running water. Cooling times are the same as blanching times.

Occasionally, if you have a glut of vegetables, it is possible to freeze without blanching. The results, however, should be eaten within two months as the enzymes present in the vegetables, which are inactivated by blanching, continue to be active at very low temperatures and will cause changes in color, flavor and texture.
Blanching times The following is a guide to blanching times:

Asparagus—2–4 minutes; eggplants—4 minutes; whole string beans or thickly cut string beans—2 minutes; coarsely sliced runner beans—1 minute; broad beans—2 minutes; broccoli—3–4 minutes; Brussels sprouts—3 minutes; carrots—3–5 minutes; cauliflower—3 minutes; celeriac—4 minutes; corn-on-the-cob—4–8 minutes; zucchini—1 minute; leeks—2–4 minutes; onions—2 minutes; parsnips—2 minutes; peas—1 minute; spinach—2 minutes; rutabagas—3 minutes; turnips—2 minutes. Mushrooms should be sautéed in butter, drained and cooled.

Freezing fruit

There are various ways of freezing fruit and much depends on how you intend to use it. Only freeze top quality fruit, just ripe. If over-ripe, purée first. Otherwise dry pack (freeze whole, without any additions), or stew gently, or prepare and either layer with sugar or cover with sugar syrup. Fruits such as peaches, apricots and pears, which are liable to discolor, should have ascorbic acid (Vitamin C) added to the cold syrup before freezing. The proportions: $\frac{1}{4}$ teaspoon ascorbic acid to $2\frac{1}{2}$ cups syrup.

Thawing

Whether to thaw food or not, and how long dishes should be left to thaw, are two problems which puzzle people from time to time. Generally speaking most cooked foods are best thawed just before reheating—it saves fuel too. Food can be cooked from its frozen state, provided you remember to allow a longer cooking time, with a slightly lower temperature, and do not try to speed things up by increasing the heat. Vegetables, indeed, taste better if plunged into boiling water straight from the freezer.

Meat is best thawed before being roasted, but if you must cook meat from frozen, choose a roast with a bone in, allow 45 minutes per pound for beef and lamb at 350°F; 1 hour per pound for pork at 400°F. It is advisable to have a meat thermometer to check that the inside of a roast is properly cooked. Raw poultry however *must* always be fully thawed before cooking so that it can cook quickly right through to the bone, thus ensuring the destruction of harmful bacteria which may be present. Some fruits, such as strawberries and raspberries, should not be thawed for too long as they tend to become soft and are much nicer while still slightly chilled.

Whatever you decide to thaw, it is best to allow the process to take place in the refrigerator overnight. If necessary, perhaps because you haven't given yourself enough time, food can be left to thaw at room temperature but cover well and do not allow to stand after thawing. A loaf of bread may be wrapped in foil and left to warm gently in the oven. Bread slices can be toasted from frozen.

Storage times

Cream and cream cheese containing less than 40 per cent butter fat separate when frozen. Heavy cream should be whipped for storing in the freezer.

Salad vegetables (lettuce, cucumber, etc.) will become limp and can only be frozen in the form of soups. Tomatoes may be frozen but will not afterwards be suitable for salads.

Whole eggs break in the freezer and if hard-boiled become rubbery. It is best to beat eggs for storage in the freezer.

Cooked whole boiled potatoes and spaghetti become soft in the freezer but roast potatoes and mashed potato toppings on such things as shepherd's pie and fish pies are quite successful.

Mayonnaise curdles after freezing.

Yogurt separates after freezing. Commercially frozen yogurt, however, contains a stabiliser. Plain yogurt freezes if you first add a tablespoon of honey.

Previously frozen food should not be re-frozen. Once thawed, it deteriorates more quickly than fresh food. That is to say, after a certain time its flavor and texture will begin to deteriorate although there will still be no danger to health. It can, however, be used for cooked dishes which are then frozen. If you want to serve food which is sure to be at its best, you should not exceed the storage times given in the column opposite:

Most vegetables—12 months raw mushrooms—1 month; cooked mushrooms —3 months; onions—3–6 months.
Most fruit including purées—12 months unpitted fruit—3 months; fruit pies—6 months.

Uncooked meats: lamb—6 months; pork—3 months; beef—8 months; ground meat, variety meats, tripe—3 months; bacon, vacuum-packed —5 months; smoked ham—2 months; sausages— 2 months.

Poultry etc.: chicken—12 months; duck— 6 months; giblets—2 months; game—6 months.

Fish: white—3 months; oily—2 months.

Cooked dishes: pies, casseroles, etc.—3 months.

Cakes, bread, pastry, etc.—6 months; sandwiches and biscuits—2 months; crisp bread and rolls—1 week; enriched bread, soft rolls— 4 months; breadcrumbs, croûtons—6 months; risen dough—2 weeks; unrisen dough—1 month; yeast—1 month.

Dairy produce: cream—3 months; eggs, unsalted butter—6 months; salted butter, cream with more than 35 per cent butter fat, hard cheese—3 months; cream cheese—6 weeks; Camembert, Brie cheeses freeze well—3 months.

All recipes serve four unless otherwise stated.
Cooking times given at the beginning of recipes apply only to cooking done before freezing. All instructions for cooking and serving after freezing are given at the end of recipes.

All spoon measurements are level.

Summer soup

1 bunch watercress
Outside leaves 2 heads of Boston lettuce
4 tablespoons butter
1 onion, peeled and sliced
3–4 potatoes, peeled and sliced
2½ cups chicken stock
Salt and freshly ground black pepper

Cooking Time: 30 minutes

Milk and cream are added to the soup after thawing and reheating to prevent curdling.
Wash the watercress but do not remove the stalks, wash and roughly shred the lettuce. Melt the butter in a pan and gently cook the onion and potato for 5 minutes, without browning. Add the stock and seasoning, bring to the boil, cover and simmer for 15 minutes. Add the watercress and lettuce and simmer for an additional 10 minutes, then purée through a sieve or in a blender.
To freeze: pour into a rigid container, cool, cover, label and freeze.
To cook and serve: thaw overnight in the refrigerator. Turn into a non-stick pan, then heat through, stir in 2 cups boiling milk and ⅔ cup cream. Taste and adjust seasoning, garnish each serving with a sprig of watercress.

Beet soup

1 lb cooked beets, skinned
3–4 potatoes, peeled
2 tablespoons butter
1 small onion, peeled and chopped
5 cups chicken stock
Salt and freshly ground black pepper

Cooking Time: about 50 minutes

Cut the beets and potatoes into large dice. Melt the butter in a large pan, add the onion, beets and potatoes and fry gently for about 5 minutes, stirring occasionally. Stir in the stock and seasoning and bring to the boil, then lower the heat and cover the pan. Simmer for 45 minutes, or until tender. Rub the soup through a sieve or purée in a blender.
To freeze: turn into a rigid container, cool, cover, label and freeze.
To serve: thaw overnight in the refrigerator. Turn into a saucepan and reheat gently. Taste and adjust seasoning. Serve piping hot. Stir a spoonful of heavy cream into the center of each serving if desired.

Chinese cabbage and pepper soup

2 tablespoons oil
4 tablespoons butter
½ lb green peppers, seeded, cored
and diced
2 onions, peeled and chopped
½ head Chinese cabbage or celery
cabbage, shredded
4 tablespoons flour
2 cups chicken stock
Salt and freshly ground black pepper

Cooking Time: 35 minutes

Heat the oil in a saucepan, then add the butter. When it has melted, add the peppers, onion and Chinese cabbage and cook gently for 5 minutes. Blend in the flour and cook for 1 minute. Gradually stir in the stock and bring to the boil. Season and simmer, covered, for 30 minutes or until the vegetables are cooked. Purée the soup in a blender or force through a sieve.
To freeze: turn into a rigid container, cool, cover, label and freeze.
To cook and serve: thaw overnight in the refrigerator. Turn the soup into a saucepan with 2 cups milk and heat through. Taste and adjust seasoning and just before serving, stir in 3 tablespoons cream.

Quick pea soup

2 tablespoons bacon fat
3 large scallions, peeled and chopped
Outside leaves of a Boston lettuce,
roughly shredded
1 lb frozen peas
4⅓ cups stock or water
Salt and freshly ground black pepper

Cooking Time: about 10 minutes

Melt the bacon fat in a pan, add the scallions and lettuce leaves and cook for 2 minutes. Add the peas, stock and seasoning, bring to the boil and simmer gently for about 5 minutes. Sieve, or purée in a blender.
To freeze: turn into a rigid container, cool, cover, label and freeze.
To serve: thaw overnight in the refrigerator. Place in a non-stick saucepan and reheat gently, taste and adjust seasoning, stir in 3 tablespoons cream and pour into bowls. Garnish with croûtons, if desired.

Iced Spanish soup

5 tomatoes, skinned and seeded
1 large onion, peeled
1 large green pepper, seeds and
pith removed
Half a cucumber
3 small cloves garlic
2 tablespoons chopped parsley
2 slices white bread without the crusts
Salt and freshly ground black pepper
2 tablespoons wine vinegar
2 tablespoons oil
A few drops Tabasco sauce
1¼ cups iced water

Make this soup when the tomatoes are at their most plentiful and cheap.
Place all the ingredients together to purée through a sieve or in a blender until smooth (place in the blender in two or three batches). Turn into a bowl and mix well.
To freeze: turn into a rigid container, cover, label and freeze.
To serve: thaw completely at room temperature, about 8 hours, stir thoroughly and spoon into serving bowls. Place an ice cube in the center of each bowl. Serve very cold, with small separate bowls of chopped cucumber, onion, tomato, green pepper, and fried bread croûtons.

Leek and artichoke soup; Iced Spanish soup

Leek and artichoke soup

1½ lb Jerusalem artichokes
2 tablespoons butter
½ lb leeks, washed and sliced
3¾ cups stock
Salt and freshly ground black pepper
Bay leaf

Cooking Time: about 50 minutes

Put the artichokes in a pan and cover with cold water, bring to the boil, cover and simmer for 15 minutes, then drain well and peel. Rinse out the pan and melt the butter in it, add the leeks and cook for 2 to 3 minutes, add the artichokes, stock, seasoning and bay leaf, cover and simmer for about 30 minutes. Remove the bay leaf and purée through a sieve or in a blender.
To freeze: turn into a rigid container, cool, cover, label and freeze.
To serve: thaw at room temperature for about 8 hours. Place in a saucepan with 1¼ cups milk and bring to the boil, stirring. Taste and adjust seasoning. Serve garnished with mint, if desired.

Vichyssoise

1½ lb leeks
4 tablespoons butter
½ lb onions, peeled and chopped
4 potatoes, peeled and diced
5 cups chicken stock
1 teaspoon salt
Freshly ground black pepper

Cooking Time: about 1 hour

Trim the tops of the leeks to within 1 inch of the white stem and cut off the roots. Slice lengthwise through the center and wash thoroughly in cold water; shred. Melt the butter in a large pan, add the onion and the leeks, cover and cook gently for about 10 minutes. Add the potatoes and cook for another 10 minutes, then stir in the stock and seasoning, cover and simmer for 30 to 40 minutes. Purée the soup in a blender, or sieve. Taste and adjust seasoning, leave to cool.
To freeze: turn into a rigid container, cover, label and freeze.
To serve: thaw at room temperature for about 8 hours or overnight in the refrigerator. Turn into a saucepan, preferably non-stick, and reheat. Remove from heat, stir in ⅔ cup cream, sprinkle with parsley and serve. For a special occasion, serve this soup cold—stir thoroughly when thawed, then stir in the cream and sprinkle with parsley, or a few snipped chives.
Serves 6

Quick pea soup; Vichyssoise

Cheese straws

1¾ cups flour
½ teaspoon salt
Pinch pepper
4 tablespoons butter
1 chicken bouillon cube
1 cup grated Cheddar cheese
½ cup grated Parmesan cheese
2 egg yolks
Cold water

Sift the flour, salt and pepper into a bowl. Add the butter, cut into small pieces, with the crumbled bouillon cube and rub in until the flour resembles breadcrumbs. Add the cheeses with the egg yolks and stir well, add enough cold water to make a firm dough.

Roll out on a floured surface to ¼ inch thickness. Trim the edges to make a neat square or rectangle then cut into straws each about ¼ inch wide and 2½ inches long. Re-roll the trimmings and cut out 6 or 8 circles about 3 inches in diameter, then cut out the centers with a 2 inch cutter to form rings.

To freeze: lay the straws and rings on a baking sheet or flat dish and open freeze. Pack in a rigid container, seal, label and return to freezer.

To cook: place on baking sheets and bake in a moderately hot oven (400°F) for 15 minutes or until golden brown. Cool on a wire rack for 10 minutes, then thread the straws through the rings.
Makes about 80

Party small ham quiches

For the pastry:
1¾ cups flour
½ teaspoon salt
4 tablespoons butter
4 tablespoons lard
2 tablespoons water

For the filling:
1 shallot, peeled and chopped
1 tablespoon butter
¼ lb ham, finely chopped
¾ cup grated Gruyère cheese
2 eggs
6 tablespoons light cream
2 teaspoons chopped chives
Salt and freshly ground black pepper

Cooking Time: 40 minutes
Oven: 375°F, then reduce to 325°F

Make the pastry in the usual way (see Leek and Ham Quiche, page 48). Roll out the dough on a floured surface and cut out 20 circles large enough to line muffin tins. Press the circles into the tins, line them with wax paper and dried beans and bake in the center of a moderately hot oven for 15 minutes. Remove paper and beans. Reduce oven temperature to warm.

Place the shallot in a small pan with the butter and cook gently for about 5 minutes. Mix shallot with the ham and divide the mixture between the pastry cases, sprinkle a little cheese in each.

Blend together the eggs, cream, chives and seasoning, spoon the mixture into the cases.

Bake in a warm oven for about 20 minutes or until the filling is set. Remove from tins.

To freeze: cool, pack in a plastic bag, seal, label and freeze.

To serve: place in a moderate oven (350°F) for 15 to 20 minutes. Serve hot.

Cheese straws; Party small ham quiches; Smoked haddock pâté

Smoked haddock pâté

1 lb smoked haddock fillet
4–6 tablespoons butter
⅔ cup heavy cream
⅔ cup light cream
3 hard-boiled eggs, finely chopped
Salt and freshly ground black pepper

Line broiler pan with foil, lay on the haddock fillet and dot with butter, broil on both sides for about 10 minutes or until the fish flakes easily. Remove the skin and any bones from the haddock and put in an electric blender with any cooking juices and the butter. Reduce to a purée and turn into a bowl. Whisk the two creams together then fold in the fish purée and hard-boiled eggs. Season well and turn into a foil dish and smooth the top.
To freeze: Cool, cover and label, then freeze.
To serve: Thaw overnight in the refrigerator and serve with hot French bread or toast.
Serves 6.

Scallops in shells

¼ lb scallops
¼ lb haddock
⅔ cup milk or dry white wine
Slice of onion
Sprig of parsley
Bay leaf
4 tablespoons butter
6 tablespoons flour
2 cups milk
½ cup grated cheese
Salt and freshly ground black pepper
Mashed potato with 1½ lb potatoes

Cooking Time: about 15 minutes

Rinse and slice the scallops. Cut the haddock into small pieces and remove any skin and bone. Place the fish in a pan with the milk or wine, onion, parsley, bay leaf, bring to the boil, simmer for 5 minutes. Drain and keep the liquid on one side. Melt the butter, add the flour and cook for a minute, stir in the fish liquid and milk and bring to the boil, stirring. Add the cheese, scallops and haddock and season well.

Divide the fish sauce between 4–6 scallop shells, or individual ovenproof dishes, and pipe the mashed potato in a border around the edge of each dish.

To freeze: open freeze, then pack in plastic bags, seal and label and return to the freezer.

To cook: take from the freezer, remove the bags, and either cook at once in a hot oven (425°F) for about 1 hour, or thaw in the refrigerator for about 8 hours and then reheat in a hot oven for about 15 minutes.

Salmon and egg mousse

⅓ oz gelatin
6 tablespoons water
⅔ cup condensed consommé
6 oz salmon
3 hard-boiled eggs
⅔ cup mayonnaise
⅔ cup heavy cream, whipped
Salt and freshly ground black pepper
1 tablespoon chopped parsley

An ideal way of using up the last of the fresh salmon left over from a dinner party.

Put the gelatin in a bowl with the water, leave to soak for 5 minutes. Stand over a bowl of simmering water and stir until gelatin is dissolved. Add to undiluted consommé. Flake the salmon and remove any pieces of skin and bones. Finely chop the eggs, place in a bowl with the salmon, mayonnaise, cream and three-quarters of the consommé mixture and mix together well, taste and season. Pour into a quart dish and leave until set. Add the parsley to the remaining consommé and pour over the mousse, leave until set.

To freeze: cover dish with foil, label and freeze.

To serve: thaw overnight in the refrigerator. Decorate with slices of hard-boiled egg.

Kipper mousse

10 oz kipper fillets
Butter
1¼ cups heavy cream
2 tablespoons lemon juice
Pinch cayenne

Place the kipper fillets, skin side up, in a baking dish, dot with butter and heat through under the broiler. Reserve the cooking butter.

Remove all the dark skin and bones from the kipper fillets and pass through a sieve, or place them in a blender, with the cream, the reserved butter and the lemon juice. Blend until smooth, add cayenne to taste.

Turn into 6 individual ramekin dishes.

To freeze: cover, label and freeze.

To serve: thaw overnight in the refrigerator. Garnish each dish with slices of stuffed olive and serve with hot toast.

Serves 6

Scallops in shells; Kipper mousse; Salmon and egg mousse; Taramasalata

Taramasalata

2 slices crustless white bread
¼ cup cold milk
6 oz jar smoked cod's roe
1 clove garlic, crushed
9 tablespoons oil
2 tablespoons lemon juice
Salt and freshly ground black pepper

Soak the bread in the milk and squeeze dry. Blend all the ingredients together, taste and adjust seasoning.
To freeze: turn into a small foil dish, cover, label and freeze.
To serve: thaw overnight in the refrigerator and serve with lemon wedges and hot toast or French bread.

Avocado and onion dip

2 avocados
Scant ½ cup cream cheese
3 tablespoons lemon juice
¼ small onion, peeled and very
finely chopped
Freshly ground black pepper

Cut the avocados in half and remove the pits, scoop out the flesh, put it in a bowl and mash well with a fork. Add the remaining ingredients and stir until well blended.
To freeze: place in a small rigid container, cover, label and freeze.
To serve: thaw at room temperature for 4 to 5 hours, turn into a bowl and serve with potato chips, stalks of celery or carrot or small sausages.

Garlic bread

2 cloves garlic
½ teaspoon salt
Freshly ground black pepper
¼ lb (1 stick) butter
1 teaspoon chopped dried thyme and basil
1 teaspoon chopped parsley
1 loaf French bread

Crush the garlic with the salt to a smooth paste and put in a bowl with the pepper, butter and herbs. Cream well. Cut the loaf along in 1 inch slices to within ½ inch of the bottom. Spread the slices on each side with the garlic butter and press together again. Wrap in foil.
To freeze: label and freeze.
To cook: thaw at room temperature for 3 to 4 hours, then heat in a moderately hot oven (400°F) for 12 to 15 minutes, still in foil, until hot and crisp.

Grapefruit and melon refresher

1 small ripe melon
1 grapefruit, peeled and segmented
2 tablespoons lime juice
¼ cup sugar

Halve the melon and remove the seeds. Peel the melon halves, cut the flesh into cubes and place in a rigid container with the grapefruit segments, lime juice and sugar. Leave to stand for 1 hour.
To freeze: cover, label and freeze.
To serve: thaw in the refrigerator overnight. Serve in 4 wine glasses.

Canadian style pâté

1 lb salt belly of pork
½ lb lean pork
¼ lb pigs' liver
1 onion, peeled
2 cloves garlic, crushed
A little salt
Freshly ground black pepper
1 tablespoon chopped parsley
3 tablespoons sherry
5 slices Canadian style bacon

Cooking Time: 1½ to 2 hours
Oven: 325°F

Remove any rind and bones from the belly of pork and cut into small pieces, grind into a bowl with the lean pork, liver and onion. Add the garlic, seasoning, parsley and sherry, mix well together. Line the base and sides of an ovenproof dish with bacon, spread in the pork mixture, cover with a piece of foil, stand in a dish of water and bake in a warm oven for 1½ to 2 hours.
To freeze: cool completely, then turn out and wrap in a double thickness of foil, put in a plastic bag, seal, label and freeze.
To serve: thaw in the refrigerator overnight, or for 6 hours at room temperature. Serve with hot toast or French bread.

Grapefruit and melon refresher; Avocado and onion dip; Canadian style pâté; Garlic bread

Basic Scotch mince; Savory mince pies; Cottage pie; Curry pies

Savory mince pies

1 portion Basic Scotch mince (see right)
Shortcrust pastry made with 2⅔ cups flour
(see page 48)

Place the mince in a bowl and make sure it is cold. Roll out two-thirds of the pastry and cut into six 5 inch circles and line six 4 inch foil dishes. Roll out the remaining pastry and cut out six 4 inch circles for lids. Divide the mince between the pies, dampen the edges and cover with the lids. Seal the edges firmly with the prongs of a fork or the tip of a metal spatula. Decorate with pastry trimmings.

To freeze: wrap the pies individually in a double layer of foil, seal, label and freeze.

To cook: unwrap, glaze with milk or beaten egg, make a small slit in the center of each pie and bake in a hot oven (425°F), for 25 to 30 minutes until golden brown.

Makes 6 individual pies

Cottage pie

1 portion Basic Scotch mince (see below)
½ lb carrots, peeled and grated
1 tablespoon chopped parsley
Salt and freshly ground black pepper
1 lb potatoes, boiled
Knob of butter
A little milk

Combine the mince with the carrot and parsley, taste and adjust seasoning. Turn into a pie dish. Sieve or mash the potatoes, add the butter and milk, season to taste, spread over the top of the meat and mark with a fork. Decorate with extra potato, if liked.

To freeze: open freeze, then wrap in foil, label and return to freezer.

To cook and serve: remove wrapping and cook from frozen in a moderately hot oven (400°F) for 1½ to 1¾ hours. Garnish with finely chopped parsley.

Basic Scotch mince

2 tablespoons drippings
(melted beef fat)
1 lb onions, peeled and chopped
2 tablespoons tomato paste
4 teaspoons salt
Freshly ground black pepper
⅓ cup plus 2 teaspoons flour
4⅓ cups water
2 beef bouillon cubes
4 lb ground beef

Cooking Time: about 1 hour

Cook the beef at one go and pack in 4 portions. A meat roasting tin is ideal as this way, you can freeze until it is almost solid, then turn it out like a gelatin mold, leave until just (but only just) thawed enough to cut into quarters, pack in plastic bags, label and return at once to the freezer.

Heat the drippings in a large pan, add the onion, stir and fry over a low heat until soft and lightly colored. Stir in the tomato paste, seasoning and flour and cook for 2 minutes. Add the water and bouillon cubes with the ground beef and bring to the boil, stirring. Cook gently, stirring occasionally, until cooked through, about 30 to 45 minutes in a shallow pan and an hour for a deeper pan.

Remove from heat and cool quickly.

To freeze: as suggested above or pack in 4 rigid containers, or make into recipes and then freeze.

To serve: thaw and use as required.

Curry pies

Make as Savory Mince Pies, but when putting the mince in a bowl, stir in 1 teaspoon (or to taste) curry powder, 1 tablespoon chutney and about ¼ cup golden raisins. Freeze, and bake as Savory Mince Pies.

Makes 6 individual pies.

Italian meat balls

¾ lb sausage meat
2 tablespoons oil
¾ lb onions, peeled and sliced
1 clove garlic, crushed
4 stalks celery, scrubbed and sliced
1 green pepper, seeded and sliced
3 tablespoons tomato paste
1¼ cups cider or stock
¼ lb mushrooms, cleaned and sliced
2 teaspoons sugar
Salt and freshly ground black pepper
½ lb noodles
1 cup grated Cheddar cheese

Cooking Time: about 30 minutes

Divide the sausage meat into small pieces and roll into 24 small balls on a lightly floured surface. Heat the oil in a large pan and add the meat balls, onion and garlic and fry until brown. Add the celery, pepper, tomato paste, cider or stock and mushrooms and bring to the boil, add the sugar and seasoning. Simmer for 20 minutes. Cook the noodles as directed on the package, drain well and stir into the sauce with the cheese. Taste and adjust seasoning. Turn into a rigid container.
To freeze: cool, cover, label and freeze.
To serve: thaw at room temperature for 8 hours, then turn into a casserole, cover and heat through in a moderate oven (350°F) for 1½ hours, stirring occasionally.

Beef Oxford

2 lb stewing beef
4 tablespoons flour
4 tablespoons drippings (melted beef fat)
Salt and freshly ground black pepper
½ lb onions, peeled and sliced
2 cloves garlic, crushed
¼ lb mushrooms, cleaned and sliced
1 green pepper, seeded and sliced
2 tablespoons apricot jam
1¼ cups red wine
1¼ cups beef stock

Cooking Time: 2–2½ hours

Cut the meat into neat pieces, put in a plastic bag with the flour and toss until well coated. Melt the drippings in a pan and fry the meat quickly to brown. Add all the remaining ingredients, including any flour left in the bag, bring to the boil, cover and simmer for 2 to 2½ hours or until the meat is tender, stirring occasionally.
To freeze: turn into a rigid container, cool, cover, label and freeze.
To serve: thaw overnight in the refrigerator, place in a saucepan and reheat gently, stirring until piping hot.
Serves 6

Italian meat balls; Beef Oxford

Meat balls in sweet and sour sauce

¾ lb ground beef
1 cup fresh white breadcrumbs
1 egg
Salt and freshly ground black pepper
2 tablespoons oil
1 onion, peeled and finely chopped
2 carrots, peeled and cut into long strips
1 leek, washed and finely sliced
2 stalks celery, scrubbed and finely sliced
4 teaspoons cornstarch
2 teaspoons sugar
1¼ cups water
2 tablespoons tomato ketchup
1 tablespoon vinegar
1 tablespoon soy sauce

Cooking Time: 40 minutes

Place the ground beef, breadcrumbs, egg and seasoning together in a bowl and mix well. Turn onto a floured board and shape into 16 meat balls. Heat the oil in a pan and fry the meat balls until brown all over, lift onto a plate. Add the onion, carrot, leek and celery to the pan and fry slowly. Place the cornstarch and sugar in a bowl and gradually stir in the water, add the ketchup, vinegar and soy sauce, pour into the pan and bring to the boil, stirring. Return the meat balls to the pan, cover with a lid and simmer for 30 minutes.
To freeze: turn into a rigid container, cool, cover, label and freeze.
To serve: thaw at room temperature for 4 to 5 hours, turn into a saucepan and heat through gently. Serve if liked with ribbon noodles.

Spaghetti sauce

1 lb lean ground beef
A little drippings (melted beef fat)
2 slices bacon, chopped
2 tablespoons flour
3 stalks celery, scrubbed and chopped
½ lb onions, peeled and chopped
1¼ cups water
1 clove garlic, crushed
1 beef bouillon cube
Salt and freshly ground black pepper
¼ teaspoon dried oregano, parsley
and basil
3 tablespoons tomato paste
Few Spanish stuffed green olives, sliced

Cooking Time: 1¾ hours

Place the beef and drippings in a pan with the bacon and cook slowly until the fat has run out, then brown, turning frequently. Add the flour and blend well. Stir in all the other ingredients, except the olives, bring to the boil, cover and simmer for about 1 hour or until tender. Add the olives and taste and adjust seasoning.
To freeze: turn into a rigid container, cool, cover, label and freeze.
To serve: thaw overnight in the refrigerator or at room temperature for about 6 hours, turn into a saucepan and reheat gently. Serve with spaghetti.

European lasagne; Meat balls in sweet and sour sauce; Spaghetti sauce

European lasagne

3½ tablespoons butter
4 tablespoons flour
2½ cups milk
¼ teaspoon prepared mustard
A little ground nutmeg
¼ teaspoon salt
5 oz lasagne
1 cup grated Cheddar cheese
½ cup grated Gruyère cheese
2 tablespoons grated Parmesan cheese
1 quantity Spaghetti sauce (see opposite)

To make the white sauce, melt the butter in a pan, add the flour and cook for 1 minute. Add the milk and bring to the boil, stirring, add the mustard, nutmeg and salt. This sauce will have a thin pouring consistency. Take a 9 inch square foil dish, and put in a layer of white sauce, then cheese, meat sauce and dried lasagne. Repeat and finish with a final layer of white sauce and cheese. Do not overlap the lasagne, break the pieces if necessary to fit the dish.

To freeze: leave to become quite cold, cover, label and freeze.

To cook: thaw for 24 hours in the refrigerator, or 12 hours at room temperature. Remove the lid and cook in a moderately hot oven (375°F) for about ¾ to 1 hour, until golden brown.

Note: the sauces are more runny than usual to allow the raw pasta to cook and absorb the liquid.

Serves 5 to 6 portions

Beef curry

2 lb stewing beef
4 tablespoons flour
1½ teaspoons salt
1 large onion, peeled and chopped
4 tablespoons margarine
3 teaspoons curry powder
1 tablespoon paprika
1¼ cups beef stock
2 dried red chillies
1 tablespoon mango chutney
1 teaspoon Worcestershire sauce
1 lb can pineapple chunks
2 bay leaves

Cooking Time: 1¾ hours

Cut the beef into ¾ inch cubes and toss in the flour and salt.

Put the onion in a pan with the margarine and fry until soft, stir in the curry powder and paprika, fry for 2 minutes then add the beef, stir well and cook for 5 minutes.

Add the remaining ingredients to the pan, including the pineapple syrup. Cover and cook gently for 1½ hours or until tender. Remove the bay leaves and chillies and taste and adjust the seasoning.

To freeze: cool, turn into a rigid container, cover, label and freeze.

To serve: thaw overnight in the refrigerator or for 6 to 8 hours at room temperature. Turn into a casserole and heat through in a moderate oven (350°F) for 45 minutes. Serve with boiled rice.

Steak and kidney pies

½ lb stewing beef
½ lb ox, veal or lamb kidney
4 tablespoons flour
2 tablespoons drippings (melted beef fat)
1 large onion, peeled and chopped
1¼ cups beef stock
Salt and freshly ground black pepper
¼ lb mushrooms, cleaned and sliced
Shortcrust pastry made with 2⅔ cups flour (see page 48)

Cooking Time: 1½ hours

Cut the meat and kidney into ½ inch cubes and toss in the flour. Heat the drippings in a pan, add the onion and fry for 2 to 3 minutes. Add the meat and fry until browned. Stir in the stock and seasoning and bring to the boil, partially cover and simmer for 1¼ hours. Add the mushrooms and cook for another 15 minutes. Taste and adjust seasoning and leave to cool.

Roll out two-thirds of the pastry and cut into six 5½ inch circles and line six 4 inch foil dishes. Roll out the remaining pastry and cut six 4 inch circles for lids. Divide the filling between the pies. Dampen the edges and cover with the lids. Seal the edges firmly with the prongs of a fork.

To freeze: cool and wrap each pie individually in a double layer of foil, label and freeze.

To serve: unwrap, glaze with milk or beaten egg, make a small slit in the center of each pie. If liked, put into ovenproof dishes, and bake in a hot oven (425°F) for 25 to 30 minutes until golden brown.

Makes 6 individual pies

Beef curry; Hot spiced crêpes; Steak and kidney pies

Hot spiced crêpes

A little drippings (melted beef fat)
¾ lb ground beef
3 tablespoons flour
¼ teaspoon Tabasco sauce
¼ teaspoon ground ginger
Salt
8 oz can tomatoes
1 clove garlic, crushed
1 teaspoon Worcestershire sauce
1 teaspoon wine vinegar
8 crêpes (see page 55)

Cheese sauce:
2 tablespoons butter
3 tablespoons flour
1¼ cups milk
½ cup grated Cheddar cheese
1 teaspoon prepared mustard
Salt and freshly ground black pepper

Cooking Time: 1 hour

Melt the drippings in a pan and add the beef, fry, stirring, for 3 to 4 minutes until any fat runs out. Add the flour and cook for 1 minute, add Tabasco sauce, ginger, salt, tomatoes, garlic, Worcestershire sauce and vinegar, bring to the boil, cover, reduce the heat and simmer for 45 minutes until cooked. Taste and adjust seasoning, leave to cool.

Divide the filling between the crêpes and roll up. Lay in a single layer in a foil dish.

To make the cheese sauce, melt the butter in a pan and stir in the flour, cook for 1 minute, add the milk and bring to the boil, stirring. Simmer until thickened then stir in the cheese, mustard and seasoning. Pour over the crêpes and leave to cool.

To freeze: cover, label and freeze.

To serve: thaw in the refrigerator overnight, remove the lid, sprinkle with grated Cheddar cheese and bake in a moderately hot oven (400°F) for 30 minutes, until golden brown. Serve with a salad.

Moussaka

4 large eggplants
Salt
7 tablespoons oil
1 lb ground lamb
½ lb onions, peeled and chopped
3 tablespoons flour
1 clove garlic, crushed
16 oz can tomatoes
Pinch each dried thyme, basil
and marjoram
2 tablespoons chopped parsley
Freshly ground black pepper
1¼ cups cheese sauce (see page 29)
½ cup grated Cheddar cheese

Cooking Time: 25 minutes

Slice the eggplants, sprinkle with salt and leave for 30 minutes. Drain and dry on paper towels. Fry the slices in 6 tablespoons oil until brown on both sides. Remove from the pan and drain. Put the remaining oil in the pan with the lamb and brown. Add the onion and cook for 10 minutes. Blend in the flour, garlic, tomatoes and herbs, bring to the boil and taste and adjust seasoning. Arrange the eggplant slices and lamb mixture in layers in a buttered shallow ovenproof dish. Pour over the cheese sauce and sprinkle with the extra cheese. Cool.
To freeze: open freeze, remove from the dish, put in a plastic bag, seal, label and return to freezer.
To serve: remove plastic bag, return the moussaka to the dish and reheat in a moderately hot oven (400°F) for 1 hour.

Creamed pork

1 lb pork fillet
3 tablespoons butter
6 tablespoons flour
2½ cups stock
½ lb small carrots, peeled
Salt and freshly ground black pepper
¼ lb mushrooms, cleaned

Cooking Time: 1 hour

Cut the pork into ½ inch slices. Melt the butter in a pan, add the pork and fry quickly for 3 to 4 minutes to seal the juices, remove the pork and put on one side. Stir the flour into the butter in the pan and cook for 1 minute. Add the stock and bring to the boil, stirring, return the pork to the pan. Cut the carrots in quarters lengthwise, add to the pan with the seasoning, cover and simmer for 45 minutes. Add the mushrooms and cook for another 15 minutes.
To freeze: cool, turn into a rigid container, cover, freeze.
To serve: thaw overnight in the refrigerator, turn into a saucepan and reheat gently, stirring occasionally, bring to the boil. Just before serving remove pan from the heat and stir in ⅔ cup light cream, turn into a dish.

Lamb steaks in piquant sauce

4 tablespoons butter
1 large onion, peeled and chopped
1 clove garlic, crushed
2 tablespoons flour
16 oz can tomatoes
1 tablespoon tomato paste
1 tablespoon brown sugar
¼ teaspoon paprika
3 tablespoons vinegar
Salt and freshly ground black pepper
4 lamb leg steaks

Cooking Time: ¾ to 1 hour

Place the butter in a small pan and fry the onion and garlic for 5 minutes until golden brown. Stir in the flour and cook for 1 minute. Add the can of tomatoes, tomato paste, sugar, paprika and vinegar and cook together for 3 to 4 minutes. Taste and adjust seasoning. Lay the lamb in a shallow ovenproof dish and pour over the sauce. Cover and bake for ¾ to 1 hour until the lamb is tender.
To freeze: cool quickly, cover, label and freeze.
To serve: thaw at room temperature for 6 hours then reheat in a moderate oven (350°F) for 45 minutes.

Lamb steaks in piquant sauce; Spiced pork rolls; Creamed pork; Moussaka

Spiced pork rolls

½ lb pork sausage meat
Finely grated rind of ½ lemon
Pinch each dried thyme, parsley, bay leaf,
basil and marjoram
4 pork escalopes
2 tablespoons oil
2 tablespoons butter
1 onion, peeled and chopped
1 tablespoon paprika
1 tablespoon flour
1¼ cups stock
5 tablespoons sherry
1 teaspoon tomato paste
Salt and freshly ground black pepper
½ lb mushrooms, cleaned

Cooking Time: about 45 minutes.

Mix the sausage meat with the lemon rind and herbs, divide the mixture between the escalopes, spread flat then roll up and secure with two pieces of string or wooden cocktail sticks. Fry quickly in the oil and butter until just beginning to brown, then remove from the pan.

Add the onion and paprika to the pan and cook for 3 minutes, stir in the flour, remove the pan from the heat and stir in the stock, sherry and tomato paste. Return to the heat and bring to the boil, stirring, simmer until the sauce has thickened.

Add the pork rolls to the pan with seasoning, cover and simmer for 45 minutes or until tender. Stir in the mushrooms and cook for 2 to 3 minutes.

To freeze: remove the string or cocktail sticks from the pork rolls, then turn into a rigid container, cool, cover, label and freeze.

To serve: thaw overnight in the refrigerator. Place in a saucepan and reheat gently until piping hot, remove the pan from the heat and stir in ⅔ cup sour cream just before serving.

Frugal Irish stew

Frugal Irish stew

Large breast of lamb, on the bone
1 lb onions, peeled and sliced
2 lb potatoes, peeled and sliced
Salt and freshly ground black pepper
½ lb carrots, peeled and sliced
1 teaspoon chopped fresh thyme or
½ teaspoon dried
Water

Cooking Time: 2 hours
Oven: 325°F

Cut the lamb into neat serving pieces and trim off any excess fat. Put half the onion into a 2 quart casserole, add half the potato and then the meat, seasoning each layer well. Cover with the carrots, then add the remaining onion and finish with a layer of potato. Add the thyme and enough water to come half way up the casserole. Cover and cook in a warm oven for 1 hour, then remove the lid and cook for another hour.

To freeze: cool quickly, cover, label and freeze.

To serve: thaw completely overnight in the refrigerator, then reheat in a modern oven (350°F) for about 1½ hours, until hot through.

Lamb with Spanish rice stuffing

Lamb with Spanish rice stuffing

1 can or package Spanish rice
3 lb boned shoulder of lamb
A little marjoram
2 tablespoons drippings (melted beef fat)
1 tablespoon flour
1¼ cups stock
1 tablespoon tomato paste
Salt and freshly ground black pepper

Cook the rice according to the directions on the package. Remove from the heat and leave to cool.

To freeze: place the meat in a plastic bag, seal, label and freeze. Place the rice in a container, label and freeze.

To cook: thaw meat and rice overnight in the refrigerator. Put the rice into the cavity in the shoulder, then put the meat back into shape and secure with skewers. Place the meat in a roasting pan and sprinkle it with marjoram, add the drippings and roast until the meat is tender (about 1½ to 2 hours in a moderate oven—350°F). Remove and place on a serving dish.

Pour off all but 1 tablespoon of the drippings and stir in the flour, cook, stirring, for 1 minute over a low heat. Add the stock and tomato paste and bring to the boil, add the seasoning and taste and adjust, simmer for 2 minutes then serve with the meat. Garnish with a few sprigs of watercress.

Serves 8

Kidneys in sherry sauce

4 tablespoons butter
1 onion, peeled and chopped
8 lambs' kidneys
3 tablespoons flour
1¼ cups stock
6 tablespoons sherry
1 tablespoon redcurrant jelly
½ teaspoon salt
Freshly ground black pepper

Cooking Time: 15 minutes

Melt the butter and fry the onion until golden brown. Wash, skin and core the kidneys and cut each into 3 pieces. Add to the pan and fry for 5 minutes, stirring. Add the flour, stir in the stock, sherry and redcurrant jelly with the seasoning, bring to the boil and simmer for 5 minutes.
To freeze: turn into a rigid container, cool, cover, label and freeze.
To serve: place in a casserole and reheat in a moderate oven (350°F) for 40 minutes, or until piping hot.

Shoulder of lamb with raisin and apricot stuffing

1 onion, peeled and chopped
1 tablespoon butter
8 oz can apricots
1 cup fresh white breadcrumbs
2 tablespoons finely chopped parsley
½ cup raisins
½ teaspoon salt
Freshly ground black pepper
1 egg, beaten
Small boned shoulder of lamb
Drippings (melted beef fat)

Fry the onion in the butter in a small pan until golden brown. Drain the apricots (reserve the juice to use in the gravy) and roughly chop. Mix the onion with the apricots, breadcrumbs, parsley, raisins and seasoning and bind together with the beaten egg.
To freeze: put the stuffing into the cavity in the meat and sew up or secure with skewers. Place the meat in a plastic bag, seal, label and freeze.
To serve: thaw meat and stuffing overnight in the refrigerator. Put in a roasting pan with the drippings and roast in a moderate oven (350°F) for 1½ to 2 hours, or until tender. Serve with gravy. Use this recipe within one month.

Braised ox heart

3 tablespoons drippings (melted beef fat)
1 lb ox, beef or veal heart, washed, trimmed and sliced
3 tablespoons flour
2½ cups water
1 beef bouillon cube
2 onions, peeled and chopped
2 carrots, peeled and chopped
2 stalks celery, scrubbed and chopped
Salt and freshly ground black pepper
1 bay leaf
A little gravy browning

Cooking Time: 2–3 hours

Heat the drippings in a large pan and fry the heart quickly on both sides to brown, remove from the pan. Stir the flour into the fat remaining in the pan and cook for 1 minute, then stir in the water and bring to the boil, add the bouillon cube and stir until dissolved. Return the heart to the pan with the vegetables, seasoning, bay leaf and gravy browning, cover and simmer until tender (up to 3 hours). Taste and adjust seasoning and remove the bay leaf.
To freeze: turn into a rigid container, cool, cover, label and freeze.
To serve: thaw overnight in the refrigerator. Reheat, preferably in a non-stick pan, for about 10 minutes.

Kidneys in sherry sauce; Pork and corn pies; Braised ox heart; Shoulder of lamb with raisin and apricot stuffing

Pork and corn pies

¾ lb lean pork
4 tablespoons seasoned flour
2 tablespoons drippings (melted beef fat)
1 large onion, peeled and finely chopped
1¼ cups chicken stock
Salt and freshly ground black pepper
1 cup corn

For the pastry:
2⅔ cups flour
6 tablespoons lard
6 tablespoons margarine
Cold water to mix
Milk to glaze

Cooking Time: 1½ hours

Trim the pork and cut into ½ inch cubes. Toss in the flour. Heat the drippings in a pan, add the onion and fry for 2 to 3 minutes. Add the meat and fry until browned. Stir in the stock and seasoning and bring to the boil, partially cover and simmer for 1¼ hours or until tender; stir in the corn and cook for 2 minutes. Taste and adjust seasoning, leave to become quite cold. Place in a large strong pie dish. Make the pastry in the usual way (see page 48).

Roll out two-thirds of the pastry, cut out three ovals to line three small pie dishes. Roll out the remaining pastry and cut out three ovals for lids. Divide the filling between the pies. Dampen the edges with water and cover with the lids. Seal the edges firmly.

To freeze: wrap each pie in a double layer of foil, label and freeze.

To serve: unwrap, thaw overnight in the refrigerator or for 4 to 5 hours at room temperature. Make a slit in the center of each pie, glaze with milk and bake in a hot oven (425°F) for 40 minutes, or until the pastry is golden brown.

Makes 3 two-portion pies.

Coq au vin

Coq au vin

1 chicken, quartered, or 4 pieces
2 tablespoons butter
1 tablespoon oil
¼ lb chunk bacon
1 large onion, peeled and sliced
2 stalks celery, scrubbed and chopped
1 clove garlic, crushed
3 tablespoons flour
1¼ cups red wine
1¼ cups stock
Salt and freshly ground black pepper
¼ lb mushrooms, cleaned and sliced

Cooking Time: 1¼ hours

Remove the skin from the chicken pieces, melt the butter in a pan with the oil and fry the chicken until brown, remove and put in a flameproof casserole. Trim rind from bacon, cut in strips, add to the pan with the onion and celery and fry until soft, transfer to the casserole. Add the garlic and flour to the fat remaining in the pan and cook until brown, stir in the wine and stock and bring to the boil, season to taste, pour over the chicken, cover and cook for 45 minutes. Add the mushrooms to the casserole and cook for a further 15 minutes or until the chicken is tender. Taste and adjust seasoning.

To freeze: turn into a rigid container, cool, cover, label and freeze.

To serve: thaw overnight in the refrigerator, turn into a casserole, cover and reheat in a moderate oven (350°F) for 45–50 minutes. If liked, put into a heated serving dish.

Country pheasant casserole

Country pheasant casserole

2 tablespoons oil
2 tablespoons butter
2 stewing pheasants
½ inch slice bacon, rinded and diced
4 tablespoons flour
1¼ cups red wine
1¼ cups chicken stock
2 tablespoons apple jelly
1 tablespoon Worcestershire sauce
¼ teaspoon fresh thyme
1 teaspoon salt
Plenty of freshly ground black pepper
Little gravy browning
16 small white onions, peeled

Cooking Time: 2¼ hours

Heat oil and butter in a large shallow pan, brown the pheasants over a medium heat, turning as each side becomes golden brown. Lift out onto a plate. Quickly fry the bacon, to extract the fat, in the butter remaining in the pan, lift out and place with the pheasant. Add flour to the pan and cook until a pale golden brown. Slowly add the wine and stock, bring to the boil and allow to thicken. Add the remaining ingredients, except the onions, return the pheasants to the pan, bring to the boil, cover and simmer for 1½ hours, add the onions and cook for another ½ hour. Test birds for tenderness by piercing the leg with a fine skewer, do not overcook. Lift out the pheasants carefully and carve the meat. Taste and adjust seasoning and, if necessary, add more gravy browning to give a good color.
To freeze: cool quickly, arrange the slices of pheasant in a rigid container and spoon over the sauce. Cover, label and freeze.
To serve: thaw overnight in the refrigerator, carefully place in a casserole, making sure that the slices of meat are in the bottom of the dish, and reheat in a moderate oven (350°F). Arrange the pheasant slices and onions in a heated serving dish and pour over the sauce. Garnish with sprigs of parsley.

Chicken risotto

6 oz flavored rice
½ lb cooked chopped chicken
¼ lb cooked chopped frankfurter or sausage

Cook the rice as directed on the package, remove from the heat and stir in the chicken and frankfurter, mix well. Allow to cool.
To freeze: Place in a rigid container, cover, label and freeze.
To serve: thaw overnight in the refrigerator. Stir in ¼ lb frozen peas, turn into a well buttered ovenproof dish, cover and heat through in a moderate oven (350°F) for 45 minutes.

Chicken paprika

3¼ lb chicken
1¼ cups dry cider
Salt and freshly ground black pepper
2 tablespoons butter
1 onion, peeled and chopped
3 teaspoons paprika
3 tablespoons flour
1 lb tomatoes, skinned and seeded
1 clove garlic
1 bay leaf

Cooking Time: about 2 hours
Oven: 350°F

Put the chicken with the giblets in a small roasting pan or casserole, add the cider and seasoning, cover with a piece of foil or a lid and cook in a moderate oven for 1½ hours, or until tender. Lift the chicken out to cool, strain off the stock in the pan and skim off the fat.
Melt the butter in a small pan, add the onion and cook for 5 minutes until soft, stir in the paprika and cook for 3 minutes. Add the flour and stir in the chicken stock with the tomatoes, garlic and bay leaf, simmer without a lid for 15 minutes, remove the bay leaf and taste and adjust the seasoning.
To freeze: carve the chicken into portions, lay in a rigid container and spoon over the sauce (if liked the sauce may be strained). Cool, cover, label and freeze.
To serve: thaw overnight in the refrigerator, turn into an oven-proof dish, cover and reheat in a moderate oven (350°F) for ¾ to 1 hour. Stir in a little sour cream or yogurt just before serving.

Norfolk turkey casserole

4 fresh turkey drum sticks
4 tablespoons butter
1 package mushroom soup mix
2 cups water
¼ lb mushrooms, cleaned and sliced
¼ teaspoon dried thyme

Cooking Time: 55 minutes
Oven: 350°F

Remove the skin from the drum sticks. Melt the butter in a pan and fry the turkey until golden brown, remove and place in a casserole. Stir the soup mix into the butter remaining in the pan, add the water and bring to the boil, stirring, add the mushrooms and thyme and pour over the drum sticks, cover and cook in a moderate oven for 45 minutes or until tender.
To freeze: cool quickly, turn into a rigid container, cover, label and freeze.
To serve: thaw overnight in the refrigerator, turn into a casserole and reheat in a moderate oven (350°F) for 40 minutes.

Chicken risotto; Norfolk turkey casserole; Chicken paprika; Italian country chicken

Italian country chicken

1 chicken, quartered, or 4 pieces
2 tablespoons butter
¼ lb chunk bacon, diced
1 onion, peeled and chopped
1 clove garlic, crushed
3 tablespoons flour
⅔ cup red Italian wine
⅔ cup chicken stock
Salt and freshly ground black pepper
¼ teaspoon dried thyme

Cooking Time: 1¼ hours
Oven: 325°F

Remove the skin from the chicken. Melt the butter in a pan and fry the chicken until brown, remove and place in a large casserole. Add the bacon to the fat remaining in the pan with the onion and garlic and fry until it is brown and the onion is soft. Stir in the flour and cook for 2 minutes. Add the wine, stock, seasoning and thyme. Bring to the boil and pour over the chicken pieces. Cover and cook in a warm oven for 1 hour, or until the chicken is tender. Taste and adjust seasoning, cool.
To freeze: turn into a rigid container, cover, label and freeze.
To serve: thaw overnight in the refrigerator, turn into a casserole, cover and reheat in a moderate oven (350°F) for 45 to 50 minutes.

Chicken in cider sauce with mushrooms

$3\frac{1}{4}$ *lb chicken*
$1\frac{1}{4}$ *cups dry cider*
2 onions, peeled and chopped
Salt and freshly ground black pepper
Milk
4 tablespoons butter
6 tablespoons flour
$\frac{1}{2}$ *lb mushrooms, cleaned and quartered*

Cooking Time: 1 hour 40 minutes
Oven: 350°F

Put the chicken and giblets in a small roasting pan or casserole. Add the cider, onion and seasoning. Cover with a piece of foil or a lid and cook in a moderate oven for $1\frac{1}{2}$ hours or until tender. Lift the chicken out to cool and strain off the remaining stock in the pan, skim off the fat and make up to 3 cups with milk. Remove the chicken meat from the carcass, and cut it into good sized pieces. Melt the butter in a pan, add the flour, cook and stir in the stock and milk, bring to the boil, stirring, and allow to thicken. Add the mushrooms and cook for 5 minutes. Taste and adjust seasoning, stir in the chicken, turn into a rigid container and leave to cool.
To freeze: cover, label and freeze.
To serve: thaw overnight in the refrigerator, turn into a casserole and put in a moderate oven (350°F) for 45 minutes or until piping hot, turn into a serving dish, sprinkle with a little finely chopped parsley.

Chicken in cider sauce with mushrooms

Calpe chicken

¼ lb prunes
4 tablespoons butter
1 chicken, quartered, or 4 pieces
4 slices bacon, chopped
1 onion, peeled and chopped
1 carrot, peeled and sliced
3 stalks celery, scrubbed and sliced
4 tablespoons flour
⅔ cup red wine
2 cups chicken stock
Finely grated rind of ½ lemon
Salt and freshly ground black pepper

Cooking Time: 1¼ hours
Oven: 350°F

Soak the prunes overnight and then remove the pits. Melt the butter in a pan and brown the chicken on both sides, remove and place in a casserole. Add the bacon, onion, carrot and celery to the pan and fry for 3 to 4 minutes. Stir in the flour and cook for a minute. Add the remaining ingredients and bring to the boil, simmer for 1 minute to allow to thicken. Pour over the chicken, cover the casserole and cook in a moderate oven for about 1 hour or until the chicken is tender.

To freeze: turn into a rigid container, cool, cover, label and freeze.

To serve: thaw overnight in the refrigerator, or for 5 to 6 hours at room temperature, place in a casserole and reheat in a moderately hot oven (375°F) for ¾ to 1 hour.

Calpe chicken

Chicken with olives

2 tablespoons butter
1 chicken, quartered, or 4 pieces
¼ lb chunk bacon
12 pearl onions, peeled
3 tablespoons flour
⅔ cup dry cider
⅔ cup water or chicken stock
Salt and freshly ground black pepper

Cooking Time: 1¼ hours
Oven: 350°F

Melt the butter in a frying pan and fry the chicken until golden brown all over, remove and place in a casserole. Cut the bacon in strips, add to the frying pan with the onions and fry until brown, transfer to the casserole. Stir the flour into the butter remaining in the pan and cook for 2 minutes, add the cider and water or stock and bring to the boil, stirring, season to taste, pour over the chicken and cook in a moderate oven for 1 hour, or until tender.
To freeze: cool, turn into a large foil dish or rigid container, cover, label and freeze.
To serve: thaw overnight in the refrigerator, turn into a casserole and reheat in a moderately hot oven (375°F) for 45 minutes. Stir in 12 stuffed green olives, taste, adjust seasoning. Put onto a heated serving dish and sprinkle with chopped parsley.

Simple Devon chicken pie; Braised squabs

Chicken with olives

Simple Devon chicken pie

½ lb cooked chicken
½ lb cooked bacon or ham
¼ lb frozen mixed vegetables, blanched
11½ oz can condensed mushroom soup
Shortcrust, puff or other pastry to top

Cut the chicken and ham into small even-sized pieces and place in a bowl with the vegetables and soup, mix together well. Turn into a pie dish. Roll out the pastry and use to cover the top of the pie, cut any trimmings into leaves and use as decoration.
To freeze: open freeze to prevent the decoration from being crushed. Put into a plastic bag, seal, label and freeze.
To cook: remove from the bag, thaw overnight in the refrigerator, brush the top with milk and make two small slits in the center. Bake in a moderately hot oven (400°F) for about 30 minutes or until the pastry is golden brown.

Braised squabs

2 squabs, split
4 tablespoons drippings (melted beef fat)
½ lb onions, peeled and sliced
4 tablespoons flour
2½ cups stock
3 tablespoons tomato ketchup
½ teaspoon fresh or ¼ teaspoon
dried marjoram
A few drops Worcestershire sauce
Salt and freshly ground black pepper

Cooking Time: 50 minutes to 1 hour

Wipe the squabs. Melt the drippings in a large pan, add the squabs and fry quickly to brown, remove and put on one side, add the onion and fry for 5 to 10 minutes until golden brown. Stir in the flour and cook for 2 minutes, add the stock and bring to the boil, stirring until thickened, add the remaining ingredients and return squabs to the pan, cover and simmer gently for 40 to 50 minutes, or until tender.
To freeze: turn into a rigid container, cool, cover, label and freeze.
To serve: thaw overnight in the refrigerator, place in a casserole, cover and reheat in a moderate oven (350°F) for ¾ to 1 hour. Serve with red cabbage (see page 48).

Smoked haddock crêpe rolls

7½ oz smoked haddock fillets
(finnan haddie)
Milk
2 tablespoons margarine
3 tablespoons flour
Finely grated rind of ½ lemon
Freshly ground black pepper
8 crêpes (see page 55)

Cooking Time: about 15 minutes

Drain off the liquid and make up to 1½ cups with milk. Skin and flake the fish and remove any bones. Melt the margarine in a small pan and add the flour, cook for one minute, stir in the fish liquid, bring to boil, simmer for 2 minutes to thicken. Add the haddock, lemon rind and pepper, taste and adjust seasoning. Divide the filling between the crêpes, fold in the sides and roll up.
To freeze: wrap in a double layer of foil, seal, label and freeze.
To serve: unwrap, thaw at room temperature for 4 to 5 hours. Melt 4–6 tablespoons butter in a frying pan and fry the crêpe rolls over a moderate heat until golden brown all over and hot through. Serve with a green vegetable.

Salmon fish cakes; Family fish pie

Smoked haddock crêpe rolls

Salmon fish cakes

8 oz can pink salmon
¾ lb freshly boiled and mashed potatoes
1 tablespoon finely chopped parsley
Salt and freshly ground black pepper
2 eggs, beaten
Browned breadcrumbs

Drain the salmon, flake the fish and remove any black skin and bones.

Place in a bowl with the potato, parsley, seasoning and one beaten egg. Mix well and shape into a roll, cut into 8 even-sized slices. Coat the fish cakes in the other beaten egg and then toss them in the breadcrumbs.

To freeze: open freeze, then pack in a rigid container, cover, label and return to the freezer.

To cook and serve: thaw at room temperature for 3 to 4 hours, then fry in hot oil for 4 to 5 minutes on each side until golden brown, drain on paper towels. Serve with a mixed salad.

Family fish pie

1 lb cod
1¼ cups shelled peas
2 cups milk
3 tablespoons butter
4 tablespoons flour
3 hard-boiled eggs
2 tablespoons mayonnaise
Salt and freshly ground black pepper
1½ lb potatoes, peeled
Milk and butter

Cooking Time: about 12 minutes

Skin and wash the cod, put in a pan with the peas and milk and simmer gently for 10 minutes, or until the fish can be flaked with a fork. Tip into a bowl and set on one side. Rinse out the pan and then melt the butter. Remove from the heat and stir in the flour, add the milk strained from the fish, return to the heat and bring to the boil. Remove any bones from the fish and add to the sauce with the peas, chopped hard-boiled eggs, mayonnaise and seasoning. Turn into a foil dish, leave to cool.

Boil the potatoes, drain, mash with milk and butter, taste and adjust seasoning. Spread or pipe a border round the edge of the dish.

To freeze: cool, cover, label and freeze.

To serve: thaw overnight in the refrigerator, then remove lid and reheat in a hot oven (425°F) for 30 to 40 minutes. Garnish with sprigs of parsley and sliced tomato.

Pizza

1½ 20 oz packages frozen white dough
A little oil

A yeast dough takes time to make, but the new frozen doughs are quick and easy to use, can be made in a quarter of the time and offer an ideal base for delicious toppings.

It is a good idea to make at least two pizzas at one go—more if you can. If you like the toppings, but find the bases a bit too much of a good thing, simply make them thinner.

Pizzas are usually round, but if every inch of your freezer space is valuable, oblong pizzas can be stacked into block shapes, which take up less room. Make them in a small jelly roll tin and cut to the size you want. Of course, there is no rule about size—make one big family pizza, or a lot of individual-sized ones. Experiment and find what suits you best. Do the same with flavors—you can always add to these by sprinkling at the last minute with a generous amount of grated cheese, or a few chopped herbs.

Let dough thaw and rise, following the directions on the package. Knead lightly until smooth then divide into 4 equal portions. Roll each piece out into a circle 8 inches in diameter and brush each with oil.

Topping 1:
3 slices salami
¼ cup tomato chutney
¼ teaspoon dried basil and oregano
2 large tomatoes, sliced

Topping 1:
Arrange the slices of salami on a dough circle, put the chutney and herbs in a bowl and mix well, spread over the salami. Arrange the tomato slices on the chutney to cover completely.

Topping 2:
¼ cup canned chicken spread
¼ cup canned deviled ham
8 oz can peeled tomatoes, drained and roughly chopped
1 tablespoon oil
1 onion, peeled and chopped
Freshly ground black pepper
6 stuffed green olives, sliced

Topping 2:
Spread a dough circle with the chicken and ham spreads. Place the onion and oil in a pan and cook for 5 minutes, stir in the tomatoes with the pepper and olives, mix well, cool and spread on the dough.

Topping 3:
16 oz can tomatoes, drained and roughly chopped
¼ teaspoon oregano
Salt and freshly ground black pepper
3 oz Swiss cheese
Anchovy fillets

Topping 3:
Mix the tomatoes with the oregano and seasoning, spread over the third dough circle. Cover with slices of cheese and arrange a lattice of anchovy fillets on top.

Topping 4:
2 tablespoons butter
4 slices bacon, chopped
4 mushrooms, cleaned and sliced
½ cup grated Cheddar cheese

Topping 4:
Melt the butter in a small pan, add the bacon and mushrooms and cook together for 5 minutes, drain and arrange on the last piece of dough, cover with grated cheese.

Leave all the pizzas to prove in a warm place for 15 minutes.
To freeze: open freeze until firm, then wrap in a double thickness of foil, label and return to the freezer.
To cook: unwrap, place on a lightly oiled baking tray and bake in oven (425°F) 25–30 minutes.

Pizzas: Topping 1; Topping 2; Topping3; Topping 4

Red cabbage

1 small red cabbage
¾ lb cooking apples, peeled, cored
and sliced
⅔ cup water
3 tablespoons sugar
1 teaspoon salt
3 cloves
5 tablespoons vinegar
4 tablespoons butter
1 tablespoon redcurrant jelly

Cooking Time: 45 minutes

Finely shred the cabbage, removing the hard stalk, and place with the apples and water in a pan. Add sugar, salt and cloves, cover and simmer until tender, about 45 minutes. Remove the cloves, add the vinegar, butter and redcurrant jelly and stir until the butter has melted. Taste and adjust seasoning.
To freeze: turn into a rigid container, cool, cover, label and freeze.
To serve: thaw overnight in the refrigerator, put in a non-stick pan and reheat gently, stirring.

Leek and ham quiche

For the pastry:
¾ cup flour
2 tablespoons margarine
2 tablespoons lard
1 tablespoon cold water

For the filling:
2 tablespoons butter
1 leek, washed and finely sliced
¼ lb cooked ham, chopped
Salt and freshly ground black pepper
1 egg
⅔ cup light cream

Cooking Time: 40–45 minutes
Oven: 425°F

Sift the flour into a bowl, add the fats cut in small pieces and rub in with the fingertips until the mixture resembles fine breadcrumbs, add water and mix to a firm dough. Roll out and line a 7 inch flan ring on a baking sheet. Chill in the refrigerator for 10 minutes. Fill with wax paper and dried beans and bake blind in a hot oven for 15 minutes. Remove from oven and take out the beans and paper. Meanwhile melt the butter in a small pan, add the leek and cook slowly until soft but not brown, then drain and put in the quiche case with the ham. Blend the seasoning, egg and cream together and pour into the quiche. Reduce the oven temperature and bake for 25 to 30 minutes or until the filling is set.
To freeze: cool, put in a plastic bag, seal, label and freeze.
To serve: remove from bag and thaw in the refrigerator overnight, then heat through in a moderate oven (350°F) for 25 minutes.

Onion and anchovy quiche

1 lb onions, peeled and finely sliced
2 tablespoons butter
2 tablespoons oil
1 clove garlic, crushed
Pastry made with ¾ cup flour (see above)
1 large egg
¼ cup heavy cream
Salt and freshly ground black pepper
2½ oz can anchovies

Cooking Time: about 1½ hours
Oven: 400°F

Put the onion in a pan with the butter, oil and garlic, cover and cook very slowly with the lid on until soft and golden; this may take up to one hour. Make the pastry, roll out, line a 7 inch flan ring on a baking sheet and refrigerate to rest. Remove the onion from the heat and leave to cool slightly. Beat the egg with the cream and seasoning, stir into the onion and put into the quiche case. Arrange a lattice of anchovy fillets on top of the quiche and bake in a moderately hot oven for about 30 minutes or until set.
To freeze: cool, put in a plastic bag, seal, label and freeze.
To serve: thaw in the refrigerator for several hours, then heat in a moderate oven (350°F) for 25 minutes.

Red cabbage; Stuffed eggplants; Onion and anchovy quiche; Leek and ham quiche

Stuffed eggplants

2 onions, peeled and chopped
1 clove garlic, crushed (optional)
¾ lb ground beef
4 tablespoons flour
1¼ cups water
1 teaspoon Worcestershire sauce
1 beef bouillon cube
Salt and freshly ground black pepper
2 large eggplants
1¼ cups cheese sauce (see page 29)

Cooking Time: 35 minutes

Put the onion and garlic with the ground beef in a pan and fry gently for 5 minutes, stirring frequently. Stir in the flour and water, Worcestershire sauce and add the crumbled bouillon cube and seasoning. Cover and simmer slowly for 30 minutes or until tender, taste and adjust seasoning. Cool. Halve the eggplants lengthwise and scoop out the centers, cook in boiling water for 5 minutes, drain well and place in a large foil dish. Fill with the beef mixture and spoon over the cheese sauce.
To freeze: leave to become quite cold, cover, label and freeze.
To serve: thaw at room temperature for 6 hours, then cook in a moderate oven (350°F) for 40 minutes or until hot through.

Cabbage and onion sauté

2 lb white cabbage
1–2 teaspoons salt
4 tablespoons butter
1 onion, peeled and chopped
Freshly ground black pepper

Cooking Time: about 7 minutes

Shred the cabbage fairly finely and remove all the hard white stalk, sprinkle with salt and leave to stand for 10 minutes in a bowl of cold water. Drain off the water, but do not rinse off the salt. Melt 2 tablespoons butter in a large saucepan, add the cabbage and cook until just tender, but still crisp, shaking the pan frequently to prevent sticking. Turn into a bowl. Melt the remaining butter in the pan and fry the onion until golden brown, stir into the cabbage and season with plenty of pepper. Cool.
To freeze: turn into a rigid container, cover, label and freeze.
To serve: thaw at room temperature for 5 to 6 hours, turn into a saucepan and reheat gently, stirring continuously.

Spinach and cheese quiche

For the pastry:
1⅓ cups flour
3 tablespoons margarine
3 tablespoons lard
Water to mix

For the filling:
10 oz package frozen chopped spinach
1 egg
⅔ cup light cream
Salt and freshly ground black pepper
¾ cup grated Cheddar cheese

Cooking Time: 40–45 minutes
Oven: 425°F

Sift the flour into a bowl, rub in the margarine and lard until the mixture resembles fine breadcrumbs, add sufficient cold water to make a firm dough. Roll out and line an 8 inch plain flan ring on a baking sheet. Chill in the refrigerator for 10 minutes. Line with wax paper, fill with dried beans and bake blind in a hot oven for 15 minutes.
Remove from oven, take out beans and paper. Cook the spinach as directed on the package, drain very thoroughly and spread over the bottom of the quiche. Blend the egg, cream and seasonings together and pour into the quiche case. Sprinkle with the cheese. Reduce the oven temperature and bake the quiche for about 30 minutes or until the filling is set.
To freeze: cool, put in a plastic bag, seal, freeze.
To serve: thaw in the refrigerator overnight, then heat through in a moderate oven (350°F) for 25 minutes.

Asparagus quiche

Pastry made with ¾ cup flour
(see page 48)
10½ oz can asparagus tips, drained
1 egg
⅔ cup light cream
Salt and freshly ground black pepper

Cooking Time: about 45 minutes
Oven: 425°F, then reduce to 350°F

Roll out the pastry and use to line a 7 inch flan ring on a baking sheet. Chill in the refrigerator for 10 minutes. Line with wax paper, fill with dried beans and bake blind for 15 minutes in a hot oven. Remove from the oven and take out the beans and paper. Put the asparagus tips in the bottom of the quiche case. Blend the egg, cream and seasoning together and pour into the quiche. Reduce the oven temperature and bake for 25 to 30 minutes until the filling is set.
To freeze: cool, put in a plastic bag, seal, label and freeze.
To serve: thaw in the refrigerator overnight, then heat through in a moderate oven (350°F) for 25 minutes.

Celery and ham mornay; Cabbage and onion sauté; Asparagus quiche; Spinach and cheese quiche

Celery and ham mornay

1 lb 3 oz can celery hearts, drained
4 slices ham
1¼ cups cheese sauce (see page 29)
½ cup grated Cheddar cheese

Wrap each piece of celery in a slice of ham. Lay in an ovenproof dish, pour over the cheese sauce. Cool.
To freeze: cover with a piece of foil, seal, label and freeze.
To cook: thaw at room temperature for 5 to 6 hours, sprinkle with cheese and cook in a moderately hot oven (400°F) for 30 minutes or until golden brown.

Lattice mince pie

1⅓ cups flour
4 tablespoons butter
4 tablespoons lard
Pinch of salt
1 egg yolk
1 tablespoon sugar
2 teaspoons water
1 lb freezer mincemeat (see page 91)
Milk to glaze

Cooking Time: 25 minutes
Oven: 400°F

Sift the flour into a bowl, add the fats cut in small pieces, with the pinch of salt, and rub into the flour with the fingertips until the mixture resembles fine breadcrumbs. Mix the egg yolk, sugar and water together, add to the dry ingredients and bind them together. Roll out the pastry and line an 8 inch pie plate. Trim the edges. Spread the mincemeat over the pastry. Roll out the pastry trimmings and cut into 6 strips about ½ inch wide and long enough to go across the top of the pie. Twist each strip once or twice and lay them loosely over the mincemeat, three each way to make a lattice. Dampen edges and press firmly to the pastry. Brush the pastry with a little milk and bake in a moderately hot oven for 25 minutes, or until a pale golden brown, cool.
To freeze: cover with a plastic bag, seal, label and freeze.
To serve: thaw at room temperature for 4 hours then reheat in a moderately hot oven (375°F) for 20 minutes, or serve cold.

Lattice mince pie; Little mince pies

Little mince pies

3½ cups self-rising flour
¼ lb (1 stick) butter
¼ lb hard margarine
4 tablespoons lard
1 egg, separated
Milk
1½ lb freezer mincemeat (see page 91)
A little sugar

Cooking Time: 20 minutes
Oven: 400°F

Sift the flour into a bowl. Add the butter, margarine and lard cut in small pieces, then rub the fats into the flour until the mixture resembles fine breadcrumbs. Add the egg yolk with enough milk to make a firm dough. Knead until blended then chill the dough in the refrigerator for 20 minutes. Roll out half the dough thinly. Cut out about 35 circles 2¾ inches in diameter and use to line muffin tins. Fill with the mincemeat. Roll out the remaining dough and cut out 35 circles 2¼ inches in diameter for the lids. Wet the edges of the dough circles in the tin and press the lids on gently to seal. Lightly beat the egg white and brush over the tops of the pies, dust with a little sugar. Bake in a moderately hot oven for 20 minutes, or until the pastry is crisp and golden brown. Leave to cool in the tins.

To freeze: open freeze in the tins, then remove from tins and pack in plastic bags, seal and label.

To serve: replace in the tins and reheat in a moderately hot oven (400°F) for 25 minutes.

Makes about 35 mince pies

Fresh mincemeat crêpes; Rich orange crêpes; Prune and apple pie; Apricot and almond tart

Prune and apple pie

½–¾ cup prunes, soaked
1½ lb cooking apples, peeled, cored and sliced (about 4 cups)
⅔ cup brown sugar
4 tablespoons butter
1 teaspoon ground cinnamon
Double batch Pastry (see page 48)
Milk to glaze

Cooking Time: about 15 minutes

Remove the pits from the prunes. Place the prunes and apples in a pan with the sugar, butter and cinnamon. Cook gently until the apples are just tender, stirring occasionally, leave to cool.

Make up the pastry and use half to line an 8 inch enamel or foil plate, spread in the filling, moisten the edges with water and roll out the remaining pastry to cover, press edges well together and flute.

To freeze: open freeze, then cover with a lid of foil, label and return to the freezer.

To serve: remove the foil lid, make two small slits in the top, brush with a little milk and bake in a hot oven (425°F) for 30 to 40 minutes, or until golden brown. Serve with whipped cream or ice cream.

Apricot and almond tart

Pastry made with ¾ cup flour
(see page 48)
16 oz can apricots
Rounded cup flour, sifted
¼ cup ground almonds
6 tablespoons butter
¼ cup sugar

Cooking time: 45 minutes
Oven: 400°F, then reduce to 325°F

Roll out the pastry and line a 7 inch fluted flan ring. Drain the apricots and arrange half over the base of the tart. Mix the flour with the almonds and rub in the butter, stir in the sugar. Cover the apricots with a layer of this mixture. Place the rest of the apricots on top and cover with the remaining almond mixture, pressing down firmly. Bake in a moderately hot oven for 15 minutes, then reduce the oven temperature and cook for another 30 minutes, or until a pale golden brown.
To freeze: cool, wrap in foil, label and freeze.
To serve: thaw at room temperature for 5 to 6 hours, mix a pinch of cinnamon with a little sugar and sprinkle over the tart, serve with plenty of whipped cream.

Rich orange crêpes

¾ cup flour
¼ teaspoon salt
1 egg
1 teaspoon oil
1¼ cups milk
12 tablespoons (1½ sticks) unsalted butter
Finely grated rind of one orange
2–3 tablespoons orange juice
1¾ cups sifted confectioners' sugar

Sift the flour and salt into a bowl. Blend in the egg with the oil and milk. Heat very little oil in an 8 inch pan. Drop 2 tablespoons of the mixture into the pan and tilt and rotate to spread out the batter. Cook for 1 minute, then turn over and cook the other side for 1 minute. Turn out and make seven more crêpes.
Cream the butter with the orange rind and beat in as much orange juice as possible and the confectioners' sugar.
Divide the filling between the crêpes and spread over each, then fold in four.
To freeze: wrap in a double thickness of foil, seal, label and freeze.
To cook and serve: thaw at room temperature for 4 hours. Heat a little bit of butter in a frying pan, add the crêpes and fry gently for 3 to 4 minutes on each side. Turn onto a serving dish and sprinkle with a little confectioners' sugar. Serve at once.

Fresh mincemeat crêpes

1 lb cooking apples, peeled, cored and
sliced (about 3 cups)
⅔ cup brown sugar
4 tablespoons butter
¼ teaspoon ground allspice
1¼ cups mixed dried fruit (golden
raisins, dark raisins, currants and
candied peel)
1 tablespoon lemon juice
A little finely grated lemon rind
8 crêpes (see above)

Cooking Time: 20 minutes

Place the apples in a pan with the sugar, butter and spice and simmer gently, stirring occasionally, for 20 minutes or until tender. Stir in the dried fruit, lemon juice and rind and leave to cool. Divide the filling between the crêpes and roll up.
To freeze: wrap in a double thickness of foil, seal, label and freeze.
To cook and serve: unwrap and thaw at room temperature for 4 hours. Fry the crêpe rolls in about 6 tablespoons butter over a moderate heat until they are golden brown. Serve with plenty of whipped cream.

Orange sherbet

¾ *cup sugar*
2 *cups water*
6 *fl oz can frozen orange juice, thawed*
2 *egg whites*

Dissolve the sugar in the water, bring to the boil and boil, uncovered, for 10 minutes. Turn the frozen orange juice into a bowl and pour on the syrup. Leave to get cold then pour into an ice-cube tray and freeze to a mushy consistency. Whisk the egg whites until thick and foamy but not dry. Fold into the orange mixture and return to the freezer until firm.
To freeze: cover, label and return to freezer.
To serve: leave to soften slightly in the refrigerator for about 5 minutes then serve spooned into glasses.

Raspberry sherbet

1 *lb raspberries*
¾ *cup sugar*
2 *egg whites*

Purée the raspberries and measure the amount of water needed to make the purée up to 2½ cups—do not mix the purée and water together. Dissolve the sugar in the water and bring to the boil, boil uncovered for 10 minutes, stir into the raspberry purée and leave to cool, then pour into an ice-cube tray and freeze until it has a mushy consistency. Whisk the egg whites until thick and foamy, but not dry, and fold into the purée, return to the freezer until firm.
To freeze: cover, label and return to freezer.
To serve: leave to soften slightly in the refrigerator for about 5 minutes then spoon into glasses.

Red fruit salad

½ *lb rhubarb, cut in* ¾ *inch lengths*
½ *lb blackcurrants*
1 *cup sugar*
6 *tablespoons water*
½ *lb small strawberries, hulled*
½ *lb raspberries*

Put the rhubarb in a saucepan with the blackcurrants. Add the sugar and water and bring to the boil, simmering until barely tender, stirring; this will take only a few minutes. Add the strawberries and raspberries and cook for another minute.
To freeze: turn into a rigid container, cool, cover, label and freeze.
To serve: thaw at room temperature for 8 hours, or overnight in the refrigerator. Stir in a little brandy to taste. Turn into a serving dish and serve with whipped cream.

Red fruit salad; Raspberry sherbet; Orange sherbet

Blackcurrant sherbet

2 lb blackcurrants
¾ cup sugar
3¾ cups water
2 tablespoons lemon juice
3 tablespoons rum

Cook the blackcurrants with the sugar and water. Add the lemon juice and purée through a strainer or in a blender. Turn into a shallow container and freeze until mushy. Take out and whisk until light and fluffy and add the rum. Return to the freezer and freeze until firm.
To freeze: cover, label and return to freezer.
To serve: leave to soften slightly in the refrigerator for 5 minutes, then serve spooned into glasses.

Lemon cream ice

1 cup sugar
8 egg yolks
¼ cup lemon juice
1¼ cups heavy cream

This is a very good way of using up egg yolks if you have been making meringues.
Put the sugar on an ovenproof plate and heat through in the oven or under the broiler. Put the yolks in a large bowl, pour on the hot sugar and whisk at once until thick and light. Put the lemon juice and cream in a bowl and whisk until the cream forms soft peaks, fold into the egg mixture, turn into a rigid plastic container.
To freeze: cover, label and freeze.
To serve: leave to stand at room temperature for 5 minutes then serve—give small portions as the ice cream is very rich.
Serves 6 to 8

Blackcurrant sherbet; Lemon cream ice

Strawberry ice cream

½ lb strawberries, hulled
¼ cup sugar
2 eggs
¼ cup superfine sugar
1 small can evaporated milk, well chilled

Place the strawberries in a pan with the granulated sugar and cook gently until soft, about 5 minutes. Purée and leave to become quite cold. Separate the eggs. Place the yolks in a small bowl and blend with a fork; put the whites in a large bowl and whisk until stiff, then whisk in the superfine sugar a spoon at a time. Slowly whisk the egg yolks into the whites. Whisk the evaporated milk in a bowl until thick and fold into the egg mixture with the strawberry purée. Turn into a quart dish and leave to freeze for at least 4 hours or until set.

To freeze: cover, label and return to freezer.

To serve: leave to stand at room temperature for about 5 minutes then serve in spoonfuls in glasses.

Note: this is a good way of using frozen strawberries.

Caramel ice cream

1¼ cups fresh wholewheat breadcrumbs
⅓ cup brown sugar
4 eggs, separated
½ cup superfine sugar
1¼ cups heavy cream

Place the breadcrumbs and brown sugar on an ovenproof or foil plate and toast under a hot broiler until golden brown and caramelized, stirring occasionally. This will take 5 to 8 minutes. Leave to become quite cold.

Whisk the egg yolks in a small bowl until well blended. In another larger bowl, whisk the egg whites until stiff then whisk in the superfine sugar a teaspoon at a time. Whisk the cream until it forms soft peaks, then fold into the meringue mixture with the egg yolks and breadcrumbs. Turn into a rigid container.

To freeze: cover, label and freeze.

To serve: thaw at room temperature for 5 minutes, then serve in scoops with cookies.

Serves 6 to 8

Strawberry ice cream; Caramel ice cream

Redcurrant and raspberry mousse

½ cup sugar
1¼ cups water
½ lb redcurrants
½ lb raspberries
⅓ oz gelatin
1 tablespoon hot water
3 tablespoons orange juice
⅔ cup heavy cream
3 egg whites

Put the sugar in a saucepan with the water and heat gently until the sugar has dissolved, stirring. Add the fruit and cook gently for a few minutes until the juice is starting to run out. Purée and allow to become quite cold.

Place the gelatin in a small bowl with the cold water and leave for 3 minutes. Add the orange juice. Stand the bowl in a pan of simmering water and allow the gelatin to dissolve, cool slightly and stir into the fruit purée, leave until almost set.

Whisk the cream until it forms soft peaks and stiffly whisk the egg whites. Stir the cream into the purée and fold in the egg whites. Turn into a strong, glass mold or ovenproof dish.

To freeze: cover with a lid of foil, label and freeze.

To serve: thaw overnight in the refrigerator. If liked, the mousse may be decorated with a little whipped cream and fresh redcurrants before serving.

Pears in fresh raspberry sauce

¾ cup sugar
2½ cups water
6 pears
½ lb raspberries

Cooking Time: about 25 minutes

Put the sugar and water in a shallow pan and bring slowly to the boil, stirring, until all the sugar has dissolved. Cut the pears in half lengthwise, peel and with a teaspoon carefully scoop out the centers. Lay in the pan and gently poach for about 15 minutes or until tender; this will very much depend on the variety of pears used. Remove the pears and lay in a rigid container. Purée the raspberries and stir in enough of the sugar syrup to make a coating consistency, spoon over the pears.

To freeze: cover, label and freeze.

To serve: thaw overnight in the refrigerator, carefully spoon the pears into a serving dish and serve with plenty of whipped cream. Serves 6

Easy lemon mousse

4 eggs
½ cup sugar
2 large lemons
⅓ oz gelatin
3 tablespoons water

Separate the eggs, place the yolks in a bowl with the sugar and beat until creamy. Grate the lemon rind finely, squeeze the juice from both lemons and add to the egg mixture. Put the gelatin in a small bowl or cup with cold water and leave to stand for 3 minutes. Stand the bowl in a pan of simmering water and allow the gelatin to dissolve. Cool slightly and stir into the lemon mixture, leave for a few minutes until the mixture starts to set. Whisk the egg whites until stiff and fold into the lemon mixture. Put into a straight-sided, strong glass mold or ovenproof dish.

To freeze: cover with a lid of foil, label and freeze.

To serve: remove the foil and thaw overnight in the refrigerator or for 4 hours at room temperature.

Strawberry fool; Redcurrant and raspberry mousse; Easy lemon mousse; Pears in fresh raspberry sauce

Strawberry fool

½ lb strawberries, hulled
1¼ cups heavy cream
¼ cup sugar
2 tablespoons Cointreau

Purée the strawberries. Whisk the cream until thick and fold in the sugar, strawberry purée and Cointreau. Turn into four strong individual serving pots.
To freeze: cover, label and freeze.
To serve: thaw in the refrigerator for 2 to 3 hours, decorate each fool with a halved strawberry and serve with Tuiles Almond Cookies (see page 83).

Bramble mousse

1 lb blackberries
½ cup sugar
2 tablespoons lemon juice
3 tablespoons cold water
⅓ oz gelatin
⅔ cup heavy cream
3 egg whites

Cooking Time: 8 minutes.

Pick over the blackberries and place in a saucepan, with the sugar and lemon juice, over a low heat, to draw the juices and dissolve the sugar, then cover and simmer gently for about 5 minutes, or until the fruit is soft.

Place the cold water in a bowl, sprinkle on the gelatin and leave to stand for 3 minutes. Draw the pan from the heat and add the gelatin, stir until dissolved.

Pass the fruit and juice through a strainer to make a purée, set aside until it is cold and shows signs of setting. Whisk the cream until it forms soft peaks, stiffly whisk the egg whites, fold both into the purée until evenly blended.

To freeze: turn into a strong, glass mold or ovenproof dish. Cover, label and freeze.

To serve: remove the cover and thaw overnight in the refrigerator, or 4 to 6 hours at room temperature. If liked, spoon into glasses, top each with a blackberry and serve with extra cream.

Fresh fruit salad

½ cup sugar
8 tablespoons water
1 tablespoon lemon juice
½ lb large black grapes, peeled and
pits removed
½ lb eating apples, peeled, cored and
sliced (about 1½ cups)
1 large orange, peeled and segmented
1 grapefruit, peeled and segmented
1 small honeydew melon, peeled, seeded
and cut in cubes
1 Charentais melon or cantaloup,
peeled, seeded and cut in cubes

Buy a quantity of fruit at a local market if you have one, if not buy when prices are reasonable. Do not buy over-ripe fruits as the freezer softens the texture slightly.

Dissolve the sugar in the water over a low heat. Cool, then stir in the lemon juice. Pour into a rigid container, stir in the fruit and mix well.

To freeze: cover, label and freeze.

To serve: thaw overnight in the refrigerator. If liked, add more fruit, eg fresh strawberries or cherries, bananas and pears, and stir in 2 tablespoons of orange liqueur.

Serves 8

Bramble mousse; Fresh fruit salad

Easy lemon cheesecake

⅓ lb graham crackers (1 pack)
4 tablespoons butter
3 tablespoons brown sugar
1 cup cream cheese
⅔ cup heavy cream
Small can condensed milk
¼ cup lemon juice

Crush the graham crackers with a rolling pin. Melt the butter in a pan, add the sugar then blend in the cracker crumbs and mix well, turn into a deep pie plate or flan dish and press into shape around the base and sides of the plate with the back of a spoon.

Place the cream cheese in a bowl, cream until soft and beat in the cream and condensed milk. Slowly add the lemon juice. Pour the mixture into the flan case.

To freeze: cover, label and freeze.

To serve: thaw overnight in the refrigerator. Garnish with a twist of lemon.

Sharp grapefruit cheesecake

⅓ oz gelatin
3 tablespoons cold water
2 8 oz packages cream cheese
6 oz can concentrated unsweetened grapefruit juice, thawed
Scant ½ cup sugar
1¼ cups heavy cream
¼ lb graham crackers
4 tablespoons butter
3 tablespoons brown sugar

Place the gelatin in a small bowl with the cold water and leave to stand for 5 minutes, then place in a pan of simmering water and leave to dissolve until the gelatin has become clear, remove and leave to cool. Cream the cheese until soft and gradually beat in the grapefruit juice and sugar. Stir in the cooled gelatin. Whisk the cream until thick but not stiff and fold into the cheesecake mixture. Turn into a lightly oiled 8 inch cake pan and place in the refrigerator. Crush the graham crackers finely. Melt the butter in a pan and stir in the crumbs and brown sugar, press over the cheesecake.

To freeze: cover with a lid of foil, label and freeze.

To serve: thaw overnight in the refrigerator. Turn out and decorate the cheesecake with whipped cream, strawberries, raspberries or grapes.

Ginger orange ring

1¼ cups heavy cream
½ lb ginger cookies

Whisk the cream until thick and use half to sandwich together the cookies and shape into a circle. An easy way is to put them in a loose-bottomed cake pan lined with a piece of foil, with a jam jar in the center, sloping the cookies slightly to fit in a circle around the jar.

Cover with the remaining cream.

To freeze: open freeze, then slip the cookie circle off the base of the cake pan, wrap in a double thickness of foil, seal, label and return to the freezer.

To serve: remove the wrapping, slip onto a serving dish and thaw in the refrigerator for 6 to 8 hours. Fill the center with orange segments, which have been mixed with superfine sugar and left to stand for at least an hour before using.

Sharp grapefruit cheesecake; Easy lemon cheesecake; Ginger orange ring

Raspberry pavlova

3 large egg whites
¾ cup superfine sugar
½ teaspoon white vinegar
2 teaspoons cornstarch

Cooking Time: 1 hour
Oven: 275°F

Whisk the egg whites until stiff, whisk in the sugar a spoonful at a time. Blend the vinegar with the cornstarch and whisk into the egg whites with the last spoonful of sugar.
Lay a sheet of baking paper on a baking sheet and mark an 8 inch circle on it. Spread the meringue out to cover the circle, building up the sides to come higher than the center.
Bake in the oven for 1 hour, then turn off the oven and leave the meringue until quite cold.
To freeze: place in a rigid container, cover, label and freeze.
To serve: place the meringue on a serving dish. Whisk 1¼ cups heavy cream until thick. Crush ½ lb of raspberries to a purée and stir into the cream, pile into the center of the meringue and decorate with ½ lb whole fresh raspberries. Leave to stand for an hour in the refrigerator before serving.
Serves 6 to 8

Hazelnut meringue gâteau

¼ lb hazelnuts
4 egg whites
1 cup superfine sugar
1 teaspoon white vinegar
⅔ cup heavy cream
3 tablespoons butter
3 tablespoons cocoa
3 tablespoons milk
¾ cup confectioners' sugar

Cooking Time: 45 minutes
Oven: 375°F

Place the hazelnuts on a tray and put into a moderately hot oven for a few minutes, tip onto a clean tea towel, rub them together well and the skins will flake off. Place in a blender and grind. Lightly brush the sides of two 8 inch layer cake pans with oil and line the base with non-stick parchment.
Whisk the egg whites until stiff, whisk in half the sugar a spoonful at a time, until the meringue is glossy. Mix the ground hazelnuts with the remaining sugar and fold into the meringue with the vinegar. Divide the mixture between the pans, spread flat and bake in the moderately hot oven for 45 minutes, then turn off the heat and leave to cool in the oven. Remove, turn out and peel off the paper. Whisk the cream until thick. Melt the butter in a small saucepan, stir in the cocoa and cook gently for 1 minute, stir in the milk and confectioners' sugar. Mix well to a thick spreading consistency and spread over one half of the meringue, spread the cream on the other half and sandwich together.
To freeze: open freeze, then pack in a large rigid plastic container, cover, label and return to the freezer.
To serve: place on a serving dish and thaw for at least 12 hours in the refrigerator. Dust with a little confectioners' sugar and decorate with chocolate flake before serving.
Serves 8

Ginger and pineapple meringue gâteau; Raspberry pavlova; Hazelnut meringue gâteau

Ginger and pineapple meringue gâteau

4 egg whites
½ cup superfine sugar
⅔ cup brown sugar
1¼ cups heavy cream
1 cup canned crushed pineapple, drained
2–3 pieces ginger, finely chopped

Cooking Time: 3–4 hours
Oven: 225°F

Line two large baking trays with non-stick baking paper or well greased wax paper. On one baking tray, mark out a circle 8 inches in diameter. On the other, mark one circle 7 inches and another 6 inches in diameter; use plates and saucers as guides. Whisk the egg whites with a whisk until they form peaks then add both the sugars in spoonfuls, whisking well after each addition. Divide the mixture between the marked circles and spread it out to cover.

Bake in a very cool oven for 3 to 4 hours, or until the meringues are firm to touch and dried out. Remove from the oven, leave to cool and peel off the paper. Whisk the cream until thick and fold in the pineapple and ginger. Spread half the cream on the largest piece of meringue, then cover with the next size of meringue, cover with the remaining cream and put the small meringue on top.

To freeze: open freeze, then pack in a large rigid plastic container (meringue is brittle when frozen), cover, label and return to freezer.

To serve: place on a serving dish and thaw in the refrigerator for at least 12 hours.

Serves 6 to 8

Chocolate simpkins; Chocolate and coffee torte; Special chocolate dessert cake

Chocolate simpkins

5 oz semi-sweet chocolate
2 eggs, separated
¼ cup sugar
⅔ cup heavy cream
½ cup glacé fruits, chopped
A little Cointreau to taste

Break the chocolate into small pieces, place in a bowl, stand over a pan of simmering water and leave until melted. Do not allow the chocolate to get too hot. Coat the insides of 6 small, strong molds or paper cupcake cases with the chocolate, using the handle of a teaspoon to make a smooth, even coating and leave to set.

Separate the eggs and whisk the yolks until well blended. Whisk the egg whites until stiff and whisk in the sugar a teaspoon at a time.

Whisk the cream until it holds soft peaks, then fold into the egg white mixture with the yolks, glacé fruits and Cointreau to taste.

Divide the mixture between the molds and smooth the tops.

To freeze: cover each mold with a piece of foil, seal, label, and freeze at once.

To serve: thaw at room temperature for about 5 minutes then gently ease out onto individual plates.

Serves 6

Special chocolate dessert cake

8 oz milk chocolate
½ lb margarine
2 eggs
2 tablespoons sugar
1 box imported Nice biscuits
Chocolate curls

This makes a special party dessert, because it looks so spectacular. Remove the ends from two 1 pound cans, wash and dry them thoroughly, then cover one end of each can with a double thickness of foil. Break the chocolate into small pieces, place in a pan with the margarine and heat gently until melted. Beat the eggs and sugar together until blended, then gradually add the chocolate mixture a little at a time. Break the biscuits into ½ inch pieces and blend into the chocolate mixture, pack into the two tins and leave in the refrigerator for 3 to 4 hours to set.

Remove the piece of foil from the base of each can, gently press out the chocolate rolls and push firmly together.

To freeze: wrap in a double thickness of foil, seal, label and freeze.

To serve: unwrap and place on a serving dish, cover with whipped cream and decorate with chocolate curls. Serve cut in slices.

Serves 8

Chocolate and coffee torte

6 tablespoons butter
½ cup sugar
Scant ⅓ cup cocoa
1 egg yolk
1 tablespoon sherry
¼ cup chopped hazelnuts
32 ladyfingers
¾ cup black coffee

Line an 8 inch round cake pan with foil. Cream the butter and sugar together until light and fluffy and then stir in the cocoa, egg yolk, sherry and nuts. Mix together well, adding a little extra sherry if necessary to make a spreading consistency.

Dip the ladyfingers, sugar side down, quickly in the coffee, arrange a layer in the bottom of the pan and cover with half the chocolate filling.

Put another layer of coffee-dipped ladyfingers on top, spread with the remaining filling, then cover with the rest, coffee side uppermost.

To freeze: cover with foil, seal, label and freeze.

To serve: thaw on a serving dish in the refrigerator for 3 to 4 hours. Cover with whipped cream, decorate with small meringues and chocolate curls and serve.

Serves 6 to 8

Plain scones

1¾ cups self-rising flour
1 teaspoon baking powder
¼ teaspoon salt
4 tablespoons margarine
About ⅔ cup milk to mix

Cooking Time: 8–10 minutes
Oven: 450°F

Sift the flour, baking powder and salt into a bowl. Rub in the margarine until the mixture resembles fine breadcrumbs. Make a well in the center and stir in sufficient milk to make a soft dough. Turn onto a floured table and knead until smooth, then roll out to about ¾ inch thickness. Cut into 8 rounds with a 2 inch cutter. Place on a greased baking sheet, brush with a little milk and bake at the top of a hot oven for 8 to 10 minutes, or until a pale brown. Cool on a wire rack.
To freeze: pack in a plastic bag, seal, label and freeze.
To serve: for speed, take the scones straight from the freezer and reheat in a hot oven for 10 minutes. If preferred, thaw at room temperature for 2 hours.
Makes 8 scones

Cheese scones

1¾ cups self-rising flour
¼ teaspoon salt
3 tablespoons margarine
½ cup grated Cheddar cheese
¼ cup grated Parmesan cheese
1 teaspoon dry mustard
About ⅔ cup milk to mix

Cooking Time: 10 minutes
Oven: 450°F

Sift the flour and salt into a bowl and rub in the margarine until the mixture resembles breadcrumbs. Mix the cheeses together and stir ½ cup into the bowl with the mustard. Add enough milk to make a soft dough. Turn onto a floured surface, knead lightly, then roll out to ¾ inch thickness. Cut into 10 rounds with a 2 inch cutter. Place on a greased baking sheet and sprinkle with the remaining cheese. Bake in a hot oven for 10 minutes, or until brown. Cool on a wire rack.
To freeze: pack in a plastic bag, seal, label and freeze.
To serve: as Plain Scones.
Makes 10 scones

Wholewheat scones

¾ cup wholewheat flour
¾ cup self-rising flour
2 teaspoons baking powder
¼ teaspoon salt
4 tablespoons margarine
About ⅔ cup milk

Make, bake, freeze and serve as Plain Scones.

Plain scones; Cheese scones; Wholewheat scones

Scotch pancakes

Lard for greasing
¾ cup self-rising flour
2 tablespoons sugar
1 egg
⅔ cup milk

Cooking Time: 10 minutes

Prepare a heavy frying pan, or electric frying pan, by rubbing the surface with salt and then greasing lightly with lard. When ready to cook the pancakes, heat the frying pan until the lard is just hazy, then wipe off any fat with paper towels.

Put the flour and sugar in a bowl, add the egg and half the milk and beat until smooth, then beat in the remaining milk. Spoon the mixture onto the heated surface in rounds, spacing well. When bubbles rise to the surface, turn the pancakes with a metal spatula and cook the other side for ½ to 1 minute until golden brown. Place on a wire rack to cool while cooking the remaining mixture.

To freeze: when cold, place on a flat surface and open freeze. Stack neatly together and wrap in foil, seal, label and return to the freezer.

To serve: spread on a tray, put in a cold oven and turn the heat to 400°F for 10 to 15 minutes, or until warmed through. Serve while still warm, spread with butter.

Makes about 18 pancakes

Moist tacky gingerbread

1⅓ cups flour
2 teaspoons baking powder
2 teaspoons ground ginger
½ teaspoon ground allspice
Pinch of salt
4 tablespoons butter
⅓ cup brown sugar
1 tablespoon black treacle
1 tablespoon golden or light corn syrup
1 teaspoon baking soda
Scant cup warm milk
2 eggs, beaten
2–3 pieces ginger, finely chopped

Cooking Time: 40–50 minutes
Oven: 325°F

Grease an 8 inch square cake pan and line it with greased wax paper.

Sift the flour, baking powder, spices and salt into a bowl. Cream the butter with the sugar and treacle and syrup and beat well. Dissolve the baking soda in the milk and stir into the creamed mixture with the flour, beaten eggs and ginger. Beat well and pour into the pan. Bake in a warm oven for 40 to 50 minutes until well risen. Leave to cool in the pan.

To freeze: remove from the cake pan, wrap in foil, seal, label and freeze.

To serve: unwrap and leave to thaw at room temperature for 3 to 4 hours. If liked, this cake could be iced with a lemon icing.

Scotch pancakes; Moist tacky gingerbread; Homemade brown bread

Homemade brown bread

2 cups hand-hot water
1 teaspoon sugar
½ oz dry active yeast

Dough:
2⅔ cups all-purpose flour
2⅔ cups wholewheat flour
2 teaspoons sugar
1 tablespoon vegetable oil
Milk to glaze
A little cracked wheat

Cooking Time: 30–40 minutes
Oven: 450°F

Make the yeast liquid by mixing the water and sugar and stirring in the dried yeast. Leave for 10 to 15 minutes until frothy.
Put all the dry ingredients in a bowl. Pour on the yeast mixture and the oil and mix with a fork, then knead until smooth and no longer sticky, about 10 minutes. Grease a plastic bag with half a teaspoon of vegetable oil, put in the dough and leave to rise in a warm place, until doubled in bulk; this will take about an hour at room temperature. Knead until it returns to its original bulk. Shape it and put it in a greased 2 pound loaf tin. Glaze with milk and sprinkle with a little cracked wheat, cover with an oiled bag and leave to rise in a warm place until the dough has reached the top of the tin.
Remove the bag and bake in a hot oven for 30 to 40 minutes, or until the loaf is evenly browned and sounds hollow when tapped on the bottom.
To freeze: remove from tin, cool, wrap in a double thickness of foil or in a plastic bag, seal, label and freeze.
To serve: thaw for 3 to 4 hours at room temperature or overnight in the refrigerator.

Orange fruit teabread

Date and walnut cake

1¼ cups boiling water
½ lb dates, chopped
1 teaspoon baking soda
1 cup sugar
6 tablespoons butter
1 egg, beaten
Rounded 2 cups flour
1 teaspoon baking powder
½ teaspoon salt
⅓ cup chopped walnuts

For the Topping:
⅓ cup brown sugar
2 tablespoons butter
2 tablespoons milk
Walnut halves

Cooking Time: 1 hour
Oven: 350°F

Grease a 9 inch square cake pan and line it with greased wax paper.
Put the water, dates and baking soda in a bowl and leave to stand
for 5 minutes. Cream the sugar and butter together until soft then
stir in the egg with the water and dates. Sift the flour with the baking
powder and salt and fold in with the walnuts. Turn into the pan
and smooth the top.
Bake in a moderate oven for 1 hour. Turn out and leave to cool on
a wire rack.
Place all the topping ingredients, except the walnuts, in a pan and
boil for 3 minutes, then spread over the cake. Decorate with walnut
halves, and leave to set.
To freeze: wrap in a double thickness of foil, seal, label and freeze.
To serve: unwrap and thaw at room temperature for 5 to 6 hours.

Apricot fruit cake

1½ cups self-rising flour
Pinch of salt
¼ lb glacé cherries
16 oz can apricots
10 tablespoons butter
½ cup plus 2 tablespoons sugar
2 large eggs, beaten
2 tablespoons milk
¾ cup golden raisins
¾ cup dark raisins
¾ cup currants

Cooking Time: 2 hours
Oven: 325°F

Grease and line a 3 pound loaf tin with greased wax paper. Sift
the salt and flour together. Halve the cherries, roll three-quarters
of them in flour and keep the remainder for topping. Drain the
apricots and chop finely. Cream the butter and sugar until light
and creamy. Beat in the eggs, adding a tablespoon of flour with the
last amount of egg. Fold in the flour, milk and all the fruit, except
the cherries for the topping. Turn into the prepared tin and arrange
the cherries on the top. Bake in a warm oven for 2 hours, or until
cooked. Leave to cool in the tin.
To freeze: remove the paper and wrap in a double thickness of
foil, seal, label and freeze.
To serve: unwrap and thaw at room temperature for about 6
hours.
Note: this is a very moist fruit cake and should be kept in the
fridge wrapped in foil rather than in a cake tin.

Orange fruit teabread

Scant cup currants
Scant cup golden raisins
Scant cup brown sugar
Finely grated rind of 2 oranges
1¼ cups hot tea
Generous 2 cups self-rising flour
1 egg

Cooking Time: 1½ hours
Oven: 300°F

Put the fruit, sugar and orange rind in a bowl, pour over the hot tea, stir well, cover and leave to stand overnight. Grease and line with greased wax paper an 8 inch round cake pan. Stir the flour and egg into the fruit mixture and mix thoroughly.
Turn the mixture into the pan and bake in a cool oven for 1½ hours. Leave to cool on a wire rack.
To freeze: wrap in a double thickness of foil, seal, label and freeze.
To serve: thaw at room temperature for 4 to 5 hours and serve either sliced with butter or just as it is.

Date and walnut cake; Apricot fruit cake

Simnel cake

12 tablespoons (1½ sticks) butter, softened
1 cup brown sugar
3 eggs
1⅓ cups flour
3 teaspoons ground allspice
1 teaspoon baking powder
2 tablespoons milk
2 cups mixed dried fruit (golden raisins,
dark raisins and currants)
¼ cup glacé cherries, chopped
2 tablespoons mixed cut peel, chopped
Finely grated rind of 1 lemon
¼ cup ground almonds

Decoration:
1 lb almond paste
1 tablespoon sieved apricot jam
1 egg white
Foil-wrapped Easter eggs

Cooking Time: 2½ hours
Oven: 300°F, then increase to 425°F

Grease a round 7 inch cake pan and line it with greased wax paper. Put all the cake ingredients together in a large mixing bowl and beat together with a wooden spoon until well blended—this will take 2 to 3 minutes. Place half the mixture in the pan and smooth the top. Roll one-third of the almond paste to fit the pan and place on top of the cake mixture. Put the remaining mixture in pan and smooth the top.

Bake in a cool oven for 2½ hours, or until cooked, then leave to cool on a wire rack. Brush the top of the cake with the apricot jam. Roll out one-third of the remaining almond paste to a 7 inch round and place on the cake, pinching the edges. Roll out the remaining paste, shape into 11 balls and arrange them around the edge of the cake. If liked, brush with a little beaten egg white and bake at 425°F for 2 to 3 minutes to brown the almond paste lightly. Cool and decorate with Easter eggs.

To freeze: open freeze, then put in a large foil container, cover, label and freeze.

To serve: thaw at room temperature for 6 to 8 hours.

Christmas cake

2 cups flour
¼ teaspoon salt
1 teaspoon ground allspice
½ lb (2 sticks) butter
1⅓ cups brown sugar
1 tablespoon black treacle
4 eggs
2 lb mixed dried fruit (golden raisins, dark raisins and currants)
¼ lb glacé cherries, quartered
¼ lb candied mixed peel, chopped
¼ cup almonds, blanched and chopped
2 tablespoons brandy

Cooking Time: 4 hours
Oven: 300°F, then reduce to 250°F

Line an 8 inch cake pan with a double thickness of greased wax paper. Sift together the flour, salt and spice. Cream the butter and sugar until light and beat in the treacle. Add the eggs one at a time, beating well after each addition and adding a spoonful of flour with each egg. Fold in the remaining flour. Add the dried fruit, cherries, peel and almonds and mix well. Place in the pan and make a hollow in the center.

Bake the cake in a cool oven for 3 hours, then reduce the oven temperature and bake for another hour, or until cooked. Cover the cake with a piece of brown paper if it is becoming too brown. Leave to cool in the pan for 20 minutes, then turn out, pierce with a skewer and spoon the brandy over the top and leave to cool.

To freeze: wrap in double thickness foil, seal, label and freeze.

To serve: thaw at room temperature for 6 to 8 hours.

Note: rich fruit cake improves with freezing. Thaw and ice this cake a week or so before Christmas.

Simnel cake; Christmas cake

Devil's food cake

Devil's food cake

¾ *cup flour*
1 *tablespoon cocoa*
½ *teaspoon baking soda*
½ *teaspoon baking powder*
¼ *cup sugar*
1 *tablespoon golden or light*
corn syrup
1 *egg, beaten*
6 *tablespoons salad or corn oil*
6 *tablespoons milk*

Cooking Time: 30–35 minutes
Oven: 325°F

Grease two 7 inch layer cake pans and line with greased wax paper.
Sift the flour, cocoa, baking soda and baking powder into a mixing
bowl. Make a well in the center and add the sugar and syrup.
Gradually stir in the egg, oil and milk and beat well to make a
smooth batter.
Pour into the pans and bake in a warm oven for 30 to 35 minutes,
or until the tops spring back when lightly pressed with a finger.
Turn out and leave to cool on a wire rack. Sandwich together with
Freezer Frosting (see page 86) and spread the remainder over the
top and sides.
To freeze: open freeze, then place in a plastic bag, seal, label and
return to the freezer.
To serve: remove the bag, place the cake on a plate and thaw at
room temperature for about 4½ hours.

Chocolate fudge cake

Chocolate fudge cake

4 oz semi-sweet chocolate
1¼ cups milk
⅔ cup brown sugar
1 teaspoon baking soda
¼ lb (1 stick) butter
¾ cup sugar
2 eggs, separated
1¾ cups flour, sifted

Icing:
9 tablespoons butter
9 tablespoons cocoa, sifted
2½ cups confectioners' sugar, sifted
Scant ⅔ cup milk

Cooking Time: 45 minutes
Oven: 350°F

Grease two 8 inch layer cake pans and line them with greased wax paper. Melt the chocolate in a saucepan with the milk and brown sugar until dissolved, but do not allow it to boil. Remove from the heat, add the baking soda and leave to cool. In a separate bowl, cream the butter with the sugar and beat in the egg yolks. Whisk the egg whites until stiff. Add by degrees the chocolate mixture and the flour to the creamed mixture, and lastly fold in the egg whites. Turn into the pans and bake in a moderate oven for 45 minutes, turn out and leave to cool. To make the icing, melt the butter in a small pan, stir in the cocoa and cook gently for 1 minute. Remove the pan from the heat, stir in the confectioners' sugar and sufficient milk to give a smooth, thick pouring consistency. Mix well and use to sandwich the cake together and pour the remaining icing over the cake.
To freeze: wrap in foil, seal, label and freeze.
To serve: thaw at room temperature for 5 to 6 hours. If liked, decorate with walnuts.

Basic Victoria layer cake

12 tablespoons (1½ sticks) butter
¾ cup sugar, warmed in the oven
3 eggs at room temperature
1⅓ cups self-rising flour

Cooking Time: 20–25 minutes
Oven: 375°F

This is one of the most useful standbys you can have in a freezer. It can take so many different fillings and toppings, can be eaten as cake or as part of another dessert, and makes a good partner for fruit. You can also vary the basic recipe by adding different flavorings.

Grease two 8 inch layer cake pans and line them with greased wax paper. Cream the butter and sugar together until light and fluffy. Beat the eggs and blend into the mixture, stirring in a spoonful of flour with the last egg. Sift in the remaining flour and turn into the two pans. Bake the cakes in a moderately hot oven for 20 to 25 minutes, or until the tops spring back when lightly pressed with the fingertips. Turn out onto a wire rack and cool.

To freeze: wrap in foil, seal, label and freeze.

To serve: thaw at room temperature for 4 to 5 hours, sandwich together with whipped cream and raspberry jam.

Variations on Victoria layer cake

Orange and lemon layer cake
Add the finely grated rind of 1 orange or lemon to the creamed mixture.

Chocolate layer cake
Replace 3 tablespoons flour with 3 tablespoons cocoa.

Coffee layer cake
Dissolve 1 heaping teaspoon instant coffee powder in the beaten eggs before adding to the mixture.

Cherry layer cake
Add ¼ cup halved glacé cherries to the mixture before adding in the flour.

Coconut layer cake
Add ⅓ cup dried coconut and 1 tablespoon milk with the flour.

Queen cakes
Add ½ cup dried mixed fruit (see page 76) and a few drops vanilla extract, and bake in muffin tins or cupcake cases for 15 to 20 minutes.

Butterfly cakes
Bake in muffin tins or cupcake cases. Cut a slice from the top of each cake and cut in half, spoon or pipe a little butter cream into the center of each cake, place the cake wings in the butter icing and dust with a little confectioners' sugar.

Coffee walnut layer cake
To a coffee cake mixture fold in ⅓ cup chopped walnuts with the flour and when cold fill and ice with coffee butter cream.

Note: all these flavors freeze well. The layer cake can be frozen filled with whipped cream or butter cream—but not with jam, as this tends to make the cake soggy.

Lemon sponge

Lemon sponge

3 eggs
Scant ½ cup sugar
⅔ cup self-rising flour
⅔ cup heavy cream
2 tablespoons lemon custard
or marmalade

Cooking Time: 20 minutes
Oven: 375°F

Grease two 7 inch layer cake pans and line them with greased wax paper. Put the eggs and sugar in a heatproof bowl over a pan of hot water and whisk until the mixture is thick, white and creamy and the whisk leaves a trail when lifted. Remove from the heat and whisk for another 2 minutes. Sift in the flour and carefully fold it in. Divide the mixture between the pans and bake in a moderately hot oven for 20 minutes, or until the tops spring back when lightly pressed with the fingertips. Turn onto a wire rack to cool. Whisk the cream until thick and blend in the lemon custard. Sandwich the cooled cakes with the lemon cream mixture.
To freeze: wrap in foil and a plastic bag, seal, label and freeze.
To serve: thaw overnight in the refrigerator or for 4 hours at room temperature, unwrap and sprinkle with sugar.

Tuiles almond cookies

Tuiles almond cookies

5 tablespoons butter
¼ cup sugar
4 tablespoons flour
¼ cup flaked almonds

Cooking Time: 8–10 minutes
Oven: 350°F

Cream the butter and sugar until pale and stir in the flour and almonds. Form into marble-sized balls and place half of them about 3 inches apart on a well greased baking sheet. Flatten with a damp fork and bake in a moderate oven for 8 to 10 minutes, until a pale golden brown.

Remove the baking sheet from the oven and leave for a few seconds then carefully lift the cookies off with a metal spatula, lay over a lightly oiled rolling pin and leave to harden. Repeat with the remaining mixture.

To freeze: pack carefully into a rigid container, cover, label and freeze.

To serve: thaw at room temperature for about an hour. Serve with mousses and fools.

Makes about 18

Note: these lose flavor quickly in a cake tin, but will keep if in the freezer.

Ginger spice cake

¼ lb margarine
½ cup golden or light corn syrup
3 tablespoons black treacle
⅔ cup brown sugar
⅔ cup milk
2 eggs
1¾ cups flour
2 teaspoons ground allspice
2 teaspoons ground ginger
1 teaspoon baking soda
1 cup golden raisins

Cooking Time: ¾ to 1 hour
Oven: 325°F

Grease an 8 inch square cake pan and line it with greased wax paper. Warm together the margarine, syrup, treacle and sugar, add the milk and allow to cool. Beat the eggs and blend with the cooled mixture. Sift the dry ingredients together, add the cooled mixture and the raisins, folding in with a spoon. Turn into the pan and bake in a warm oven for ¾ to 1 hour, or until well risen and golden brown. Turn out and leave to cool on a wire rack.
To freeze: wrap in foil, seal, label and freeze.
To serve: thaw at room temperature for 5 to 6 hours.

Freezer frosting

1 cup sugar
⅔ cup water
Pinch of cream of tartar
1 egg white, whisked

This is a good icing to use on cakes you are freezing. Put the sugar into a saucepan with the water and stir over a low heat until the sugar has dissolved. Bring to the boil and heat to 238°F, or until a small amount dropped in a saucer of cold water forms a ball. Remove from the heat, add the cream of tartar and beat lightly, until the syrup is just cloudy. Pour onto the stiffly whisked egg white, whisking all the time, and continue whisking until the mixture thickens and loses its shiny look. Use at once.

Ginger spice cake

Rich chocolate sauce

3 tablespoons butter
3 tablespoons cocoa, sifted
Small can evaporated milk
Scant cup confectioners' sugar, sifted

Melt the butter in a small saucepan, stir in the cocoa and cook for 1 minute. Remove from the heat, stir in the evaporated milk and confectioners' sugar and mix well.

To freeze: turn into a rigid plastic container, leave to cool, cover, label and freeze.

To serve: thaw at room temperature for 2 hours. Serve as a sauce with plain sponge cake, or over small choux pastry buns filled with whipped cream. It is also very good served over portions of ice cream.

Freezer frosting; Rich chocolate sauce

Chocolate fork cookies

½ lb (2 sticks) butter
½ cup sugar
1 teaspoon vanilla extract
1¾ cups self-rising flour
Rounded ⅓ cup cocoa mix
Confectioners' sugar and nuts (optional)

Cream the butter with the sugar and vanilla extract, then work in the flour and chocolate. Divide into pieces the size of a walnut and roll into balls, place on a baking sheet and flatten with a fork, dipped in cold water. Decorate with confectioners' sugar and nuts, if desired.

To freeze: open freeze, then pack into a rigid container, cover, label and freeze.

To cook: take straight from the freezer, place on a greased baking tray and bake in a moderately hot oven (375°F) for 12 to 15 minutes. Leave to firm for a minute on the baking tray, then cool on a wire rack.

Makes about 36 cookies

Chocolate crunch cookies; Brown sugar cookies

Chocolate fork cookies

Chocolate crunch cookies

1¾ cups flour
3 tablespoons cocoa
Pinch salt
12 tablespoons (1½ sticks) butter
½ cup superfine sugar
2 tablespoons granulated sugar

Cooking Time: 20 minutes
Oven: 325°F

Sift the flour and cocoa into a bowl with the salt. Cream the butter until soft, add the superfine sugar and beat until light and fluffy, then blend in the flour and work until smooth. Divide the mixture into two equal pieces each 6 inches long. Roll in the granulated sugar, then wrap in foil and chill in the refrigerator until firm. Grease two baking sheets, cut each roll into 16 slices, place on the baking sheets and bake in a warm oven for 20 minutes, or until the edges are turning a deeper shade of brown. Leave to cool on a wire rack.
To freeze: pack in a rigid container, cover, label and freeze.
To serve: remove from the container, thaw at room temperature for about 1 hour.
Makes 32 cookies

Brown sugar cookies

1¾ cups flour
Pinch salt
12 tablespoons (1½ sticks) butter
Scant cup brown sugar

Cooking Time: 20 minutes
Oven: 325°F

Sift the flour and salt into a bowl. Cream the butter until soft and then add three-quarters of the sugar and beat until light and fluffy. Blend in the flour and work until smooth. Divide the mixture into two equal pieces and roll out to form sausages each 6 inches long. Roll in the remaining sugar, then wrap in foil and chill in the refrigerator until firm. Grease two baking sheets, cut each sausage into 16 slices and place on the baking sheets. Bake in a warm oven for 20 minutes, or until the cookies are pale golden brown at the edges. Leave to cool on a wire rack.
To freeze: pack in a rigid container, cover, label and freeze.
To serve: remove from the container, thaw at room temperature for about 1 hour.
Makes 32 cookies

Coconut ice

3 cups sugar
1¼ cups water
2 pinches of cream of tartar
½ lb dried coconut
A little pink coloring

Cooking Time: about 20 minutes

Line a 7 inch square pan with wax paper. Dissolve half the sugar in half the water, add one pinch of cream of tartar, bring to the boil and boil to 238°F, or until a little of the syrup forms a soft ball when dropped into cold water. Remove from the heat and stir in half the coconut all at once. Pour into the prepared pan and leave to set.

Make a second quantity of coconut ice in the same way but, when adding the coconut, stir in a little pink coloring, avoiding over mixing. Spread over the first layer in the pan. When cold, cut in blocks and wrap in wax paper.

To freeze: overwrap in foil, seal, label and freeze.

To serve: thaw at room temperature for 5 to 6 hours.

Coconut ice

Raisin fudge

Small can evaporated milk
6 tablespoons butter
1 lb sugar (about 2¼ cups)
⅔ cup water
¼ teaspoon vanilla extract
½ cup golden raisins

Cooking Time: about 15 minutes

Butter a shallow 7 inch square pan. Put the evaporated milk, butter, sugar and water in a heavy pan, heat slowly until the sugar has dissolved, without boiling. Boil steadily to 237°F, stirring constantly, or until a small amount forms a soft ball when dropped into cold water. Remove from heat and add vanilla extract. Cool slightly and then beat, as the mixture thickens. Stir in the raisins as it starts to crystallize on the spoon.

Pour into the pan and leave to set. When firm, cut into 36 squares.
To freeze: pack in a rigid plastic container, cover, label and freeze.
To serve: remove from container, thaw in a single layer at room temperature for 1 to 2 hours.
Note: fudge makes a good Christmas present to give by hand—postage is out of the question as it is heavy stuff! Make ahead and freeze and it will certainly save time.

Raisin fudge

Easy Seville orange marmalade

Easy Seville orange marmalade

3 lb frozen Seville or other bitter oranges
7½ cups water
¼ cup lemon juice
6 lb (13–14 cups) sugar, warmed

Cooking Time: about 40 minutes

This marmalade is made from whole fruit in a pressure cooker and is an ideal way to use frozen Seville oranges. If you haven't a large pressure cooker, make half the quantity. The time to freeze oranges is between December and February—freeze them whole and use them for marmalade before the next season comes round. Put frozen oranges (do not thaw) and the water in the pressure cooker, cover and bring to 15 lb pressure for 20 minutes. Cool the pan in water to release the lid. Test the oranges for tenderness by pricking the skin with a pin. If it goes in easily the oranges are ready. Lift all the fruit out into a colander (catch any juice in a bowl underneath and return to the pan). Cut the oranges in half, remove all the pits and put the pits back into the pan, cover and bring to 15 pound pressure for another 5 minutes.

Meanwhile, slice all the orange peel shells, using a knife and fork on a wooden board, put this peel, lemon juice and warmed sugar in a large preserving pan, strain in water and juice from the pressure cooker and throw away the pits, stir over the heat to dissolve the sugar, then boil rapidly. Test for setting after 10 minutes. To do this, spoon a small amount onto a cold saucer—when it is cool, the skin that forms should wrinkle when pushed with the finger. Pour into hot clean jars, cover and label.

Makes 10 pounds marmalade.

Freezer mincemeat

Freezer mincemeat

1½ lb (about 5 cups) seeded dark raisins
¼ lb mixed peel
2 lb cooking apples
¾ lb (2¼ cups) currants
½ lb (2¼ cups) golden raisins
1 cup shredded suet
½ teaspoon ground allspice
¼ cup lemon juice
Finely grated rind of 2 lemons
1½ lb (3⅓ cups) sugar
6 tablespoons rum, brandy or sherry

Finely chop or mince the raisins. Peel, core and chop or mince the apples. Place the raisins and apples in a large bowl with the other fruit, suet and spice. Add the lemon juice and rind, sugar, and rum, brandy or sherry. Mix thoroughly and leave to stand overnight.
To freeze: turn into a large rigid container or, if preferred, several small ones. Cover, label and freeze.
To serve: thaw in the refrigerator overnight and use as required.
Note: this mincemeat needs to be kept in the freezer. Because of its high proportion of apple, it will not keep for more than a month in the refrigerator.

Egg and chive sandwiches

3 large eggs
6 tablespoons milk
1 tablespoon butter
3 teaspoons mayonnaise
2 teaspoons chopped chives
Salt and freshly ground black pepper

Scramble the eggs with the milk in the butter. Leave to cool and stir in the mayonnaise and chives. Season well.

Cream cheese and shrimp sandwiches

1 cup cream cheese
⅓ cup chopped shrimps
Salt and freshly ground black pepper

Combine the cheese and shrimps. Season well.

Sardine and tomato sandwiches

6 oz sardines, drained
2 tomatoes
Salt and freshly ground black pepper

Blend the sardines with the chopped tomatoes, season well.

To freeze the sandwiches:
Pack in layers with pieces of wax or freezer paper in between. Wrap in foil.
To serve: thaw at room temperature in the foil wrapping for 4 hours.

Black bread

Yeast Mixture:
1 teaspoon sugar
1¼ cups hand hot water
1 oz dry active yeast

Dough:
2⅔ cups rye flour
2⅔ cups all-purpose flour
1 teaspoon salt
1 tablespoon black treacle
⅔ cup milk
½ teaspoon caraway seeds
½ teaspoon vegetable oil

Cooking Time: 35–40 minutes
Oven: 425°F

To make up the yeast mixture, add sugar to water, sprinkle yeast on top. Stir well, leave 10–15 minutes, until frothy. To make up the dough, sift the flours and salt into a bowl. Add the treacle to the milk and warm slightly, then add the caraway seeds to the flour, make a well in the center and add the milk and treacle and the yeast mixture. Mix to a firm dough, put on a board, knead about 10 minutes.
Put into a plastic bag greased with ½ teaspoon vegetable oil and leave in a warm place until doubled in bulk, this will take about 1 hour at room temperature. Knead back to original bulk; this is called knocking back.
Divide the dough into 2 pieces and mold into 2 long loaves. Place on a well greased baking sheet, cover with oiled bags and leave to rise for about 40 minutes. Remove bags, brush with milk and bake for 35–40 minutes until browned and hollow sounding when tapped on base. Cool.
To freeze: wrap in a double thickness of foil or in a plastic bag, seal, label and freeze.
To serve: thaw at room temperature for 3 to 4 hours.

Lemon sausage thyme stuffing

2 tablespoons butter
2 onions, peeled and finely chopped
1 lb pork sausage meat
3½ cups fresh white breadcrumbs
2–3 tablespoons finely chopped parsley
1 teaspoon fresh thyme, preferably lemon thyme, or ½ teaspoon dried thyme
Finely grated rind of 1 lemon
2 tablespoons lemon juice
1 teaspoon salt
Freshly ground black pepper
1 egg, beaten

Cooking Time: about 10 minutes

Melt the butter in a pan, add the onion and fry until soft, about 10 minutes. Stir in the remaining ingredients and mix well together.
To freeze: put in a plastic bag, seal, label and freeze.
To serve: thaw in the refrigerator overnight, then use to stuff a turkey.
Makes enough to stuff a 12 pound turkey.
Note: fresh herbs give this stuffing a much better flavor than dried ones.

Croûtons

Cut slices of white bread, remove the crusts and cut into ½ inch cubes. Fry in shallow or deep fat until crisp and golden. Drain thoroughly on paper towels.
To freeze: pack in plastic bags, seal, label and freeze.
To serve: place uncovered, but still frozen, in a moderately hot oven (400°F) for about 5 minutes.

Mint sauce

Large bunch of mint, finely chopped
1 cup sugar
1¼ cups water

Divide the mint among the sections of an ice-cube tray. Place the sugar and water in a saucepan and heat gently until the sugar has dissolved, then boil gently for 3 to 4 minutes. Pour over the mint in the ice tray. Cool.
To freeze: open freeze until solid, then remove cubes from tray and put in a plastic bag, seal, label and return to freezer.
To serve: thaw the number of cubes required in a sauce boat and add a little vinegar to taste.

Brandy butter

12 tablespoons (1½ sticks) unsalted butter
2⅔ cups confectioners' sugar, sifted
4–6 tablespoons brandy

Cream the butter with a wooden spoon until it is soft. Gradually beat in the confectioners' sugar and continue beating until the mixture is light and soft. Beat in the brandy.
To freeze: turn into a small rigid container, cover, label and freeze.
To serve: thaw for 12 hours at room temperature, turn into a small serving dish.

Chestnut stuffing; Brandy butter; Croûtons; Lemon sausage thyme stuffing; Mint sauce

Chestnut stuffing

15½ oz can whole chestnuts in water,
drained and chopped
1¾ cups fresh wholewheat breadcrumbs
Finely grated rind of ½ lemon
1 large egg, beaten
4 tablespoons butter
1 onion, peeled and chopped
Salt and freshly ground black pepper

Cooking Time: about 10 minutes

Place the chestnuts in a bowl with the breadcrumbs, lemon rind and beaten egg. Melt the butter in a small pan, add the onion and cook gently for about 10 minutes or until soft. Add to the bowl with the seasoning and mix well.

To freeze: turn into a plastic bag, seal, label and freeze.

To serve: thaw in the refrigerator overnight and then use to stuff a turkey.

Makes enough for a 12 pound turkey.

Index

Painting Houses, Cottages and Towns on Rocks

LIN WELLFORD

NORTH LIGHT BOOKS
CINCINNATI, OHIO

ABOUT THE AUTHOR

Lin Wellford started her artistic career early, making her first sale, an ink sketch, at age 14. She studied commercial art at the University of Florida and found some success as a watercolor painter. After moving with her family to the Ozark Mountains of northern Arkansas, she was intrigued by the area's abundant rocks. Her previous book, *The Art of Painting Animals on Rocks* (North Light Books, 1994), opened a door to the many creative possibilities using rocks as a medium. She hopes to both elevate the stature of this unique natural resource and to introduce others to the joys of three-dimensional painting.

Ms. Wellford lives in Carroll County, Arkansas. She and her husband are parents of three daughters.

Painting Houses, Cottages and Towns on Rocks. Copyright © 1996 by Lin Wellford. Manufactured in China. All rights reserved. No part of this book may be reproduced in any form or by any electronic or mechanical means including information storage and retrieval systems without permission in writing from the publisher, except by a reviewer, who may quote brief passages in a review. Published by North Light Books, an imprint of F&W Publications, Inc., 1507 Dana Avenue, Cincinnati, Ohio 45207. (800) 289-0963. First edition.

Other fine North Light Books are available from your local bookstore, art supply store or direct from the publisher.

01 00 99   8 7 6

Library of Congress Cataloging-in-Publication Data

Wellford, Lin.
    Painting houses, cottages, and towns on rocks / by Lin Wellford.
        p. cm.
    Includes index.
    ISBN 0-89134-720-8 (pbk. : alk. paper)
    1. Stone painting. 2. Acrylic painting. 3. Dwellings in art. 4. Cities and towns in art. I. Title.
TT370.W46 1996
751.4'26—dc20   96-5631
                                CIP

Edited by Kathy Kipp and Rachel Wolf
Cover designed by Brian Roeth
Cover photography by Pamela Monfort Braun/Bronze Photography

METRIC CONVERSION CHART		
TO CONVERT	**TO**	**MULTIPLY BY**
Inches	Centimeters	2.54
Centimeters	Inches	0.4
Feet	Centimeters	30.5
Centimeters	Feet	0.03
Yards	Meters	0.9
Meters	Yards	1.1
Sq. Inches	Sq. Centimeters	6.45
Sq. Centimeters	Sq. Inches	0.16
Sq. Feet	Sq. Meters	0.09
Sq. Meters	Sq. Feet	10.8
Sq. Yards	Sq. Meters	0.8
Sq. Meters	Sq. Yards	1.2
Pounds	Kilograms	0.45
Kilograms	Pounds	2.2
Ounces	Grams	28.4
Grams	Ounces	0.04

DEDICATION

For my husband Klaus and our
daughters, Skye, Erika and Kira—
who have all learned to live with a
house full of rocks.

Table *of* Contents

Painting Houses, Cottages and Towns on Rocks

Introduction

For nearly two decades I've specialized in turning ordinary rocks into unique works of art. Although I literally stumbled onto this unusual art form, from the start I sensed I'd never go back to "painting flat." Maybe it's the fact that rocks are both common and free for the taking. Or it could be their solid "realness" and lack of pretension. Whatever the attraction, I've discovered that many others share my affinity for this underrated natural resource.

It doesn't take a degree in geology to know that much of our planet's surface is studded with rock. Whether spewed from the mouth of an ancient volcano, exposed by erosion or thrust upward by grinding plates deep underground, rocks can be found just about everywhere. Some break off and tumble along rivers and streams, ending up smooth and round. My first book, *The Art of Painting Animals on Rocks*, shows techniques for transforming rounded river rocks into lifelike creatures of all kinds. But there are many more types of rock, and just as many exciting things you can do with them.

Rocks come in every size, shape and texture imaginable. Some feature sharp edges, pointy ends and flat sides. Others are chunky, with odd bumps and peculiar angles. They accumulate along roadsides and ditches, cropping up in vacant lots and farm fields, perhaps even in your own backyard.

With some practice and a few inexpensive supplies, these same rocks can be turned into charming cottages,

Your rock buildings can be used to create charming village scenes, or they can be put to practical use such as these bookends.

Victorian mansions, churches, village shops and much more. Little rock buildings are intriguing to look at and great fun to paint. Display them singly, in small groups or as part of a village. They make charming paperweights, doorstops, even bookends. Try tucking a tiny "gravel" village into the base of a houseplant. Or arrange a whimsical

vignette mounted on a larger stone. Maybe you'll discover more ways to use or display them. The options are endless.

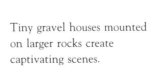

Tiny gravel houses mounted on larger rocks create captivating scenes.

GETTING STARTED

Rocks can be found nearly everywhere. They are so much a part of the landscape that it's likely you never paid much attention to them. Sandstone, granite, ceramic-like chert, shale and limestone are just a few of the myriad kinds of rocks waiting to be transformed, using nothing more than your imagination and a bit of paint. Once you've tried it, you'll never look at rocks in quite the same way. And you may discover that hunting for the perfect rock to paint is a big part of the fun.

Rock Hunting Tips

Finding potential cottage rocks may be as simple as wandering around outside your house. That's where I found the rock I used to create the striking pink fantasy of a Victorian mansion on page 108.

Other likely places include roadsides and construction sites where exposed rocks have tumbled into convenient piles. Dirt roads subject to frequent grading are often lined with rocks in assorted sizes and shapes. Lake shores also make promising collection sites, as do some creek banks and streambeds. Once you begin paying attention you'll probably be amazed at how many kinds of rocks there are in your immediate vicinity.

Not all rocks are suitable for painting, however. Poor choices include very rough or porous stones, and ones pocked with lots of little holes. Aggregate rocks, those made up of tiny pebbles stuck together, are usually too bumpy. Any surface that makes fine lines and details hard to paint should be avoided.

Shape. Beginners should concentrate on looking for simple geometric shapes. But whether you want to try your hand at a basic cottage or something more elaborate, all the rocks for buildings share a few traits. First and foremost they need to have a flat bottom. Houses must sit solidly without tipping or rocking. Next, look for vertical sides that suggest straight walls. However, if the front and one side are perfect but the other side slants, you can try camouflaging the unwanted slope with a shrub.

Other problems include deep dents or depressions, odd lines and fractures that mar the painting surface. Often these can be corrected with wood filler. Sometimes flaws can be incorporated into your design and turned into assets. The back side of the rock is the least important. You may elect to paint fewer details there, or to leave that side unpainted altogether.

Size. Size-wise, you have plenty of options. Every project presented in this book can be done using rocks that range from the tiniest "gravel cottages" all the way up to as big a rock as you care to wrestle onto your painting table.

For beginners I suggest selecting a stone around the size of a clenched fist. If you're planning to create an entire village, collect rocks that fall roughly within the same scale. A simple guide is to make sure that the same size front door will look right on all of them. This ensures your various buildings will "fit" together as a group.

Imperfections. As you rock hunt, don't expect perfection. Rocks rarely conform to the neat, tidy shapes you

Shapes to Look For . . .

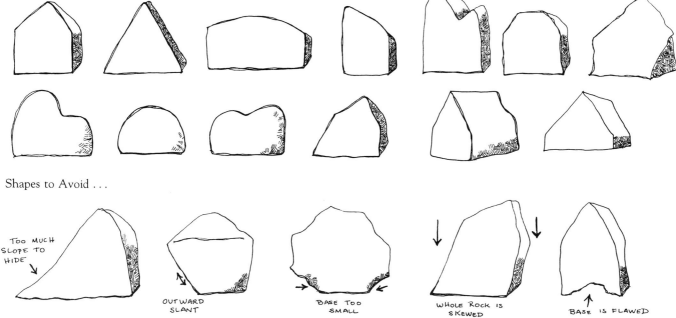

Shapes to Avoid . . .

Painting Houses, Cottages and Towns on Rocks

may have in mind. If a roofline is crooked, or the sides are far from plumb, consider such imperfections part of the charm of this medium. Every once in a while you will come across a truly ideal rock, and that is a thrill. More commonly, though, you will have to compromise. If not, you're likely to do a lot more hunting and a lot less painting.

In any art the human eye is eager to recognize something familiar. Adding a couple of windows and a door to even the poorest of rocks will automatically make it look like a cottage. As you experiment you'll discover how easy it is to conceal problem areas by simply painting over them. Remember, too, that many rocks offer more than one possibility. Try turning any promising stone over and around to see which view works best.

While straight, symmetrical walls are desirable for most styles of buildings, "skewed" angles or rounded tops can make charming "gnome homes" or rickety but quaint cottages. As you become more accomplished, you will begin to see how odd protuberances, bumps, knobs and jutting angles can be turned into porches, bay windows, overhangs, dormers, chimneys and other architectural elements. Imagination is like a muscle—the more it's used, the stronger and more supple it will become. Explore any rock that appeals to you and practice visualizing what it might look like with a few details painted in.

Have Fun. Look over the various projects presented in this book before you begin collecting your rocks. Most of all, hunting for rocks should be something of an adventure. Bring along a playful attitude and sense of discovery. After all, you never know what you're going to find.

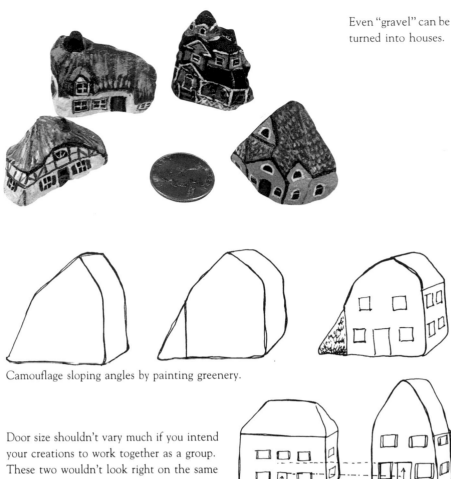

Even "gravel" can be turned into houses.

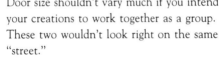

Camouflage sloping angles by painting greenery.

Door size shouldn't vary much if you intend your creations to work together as a group. These two wouldn't look right on the same "street."

The author at a prime rock-hunting site.

SUPPLIES

Once you've gathered some potential cottage rocks, there are a few inexpensive, easy-to-find supplies you'll need.

Paints

I use acrylic craft paint because it comes in so many colors and the consistency is close to ideal right out of the bottle. However, if you have tube acrylics on hand, they'll work fine, too. Even oil paints or those tiny bottles of model paint can be used, although these require turpentine or other solvents for thinning and cleanup while acrylics need only water. People who use a lot of paint should consider buying high-gloss or semigloss acrylic house and trim type paint from a hardware store. It's far cheaper by the pint or quart than the 2-ounce (59 milliliter) craft paint, and the quality is usually better. There isn't the same extensive color selection, but I buy my black and white paint this way and use a large syringe to transfer it into empty craft paint bottles for easy access.

Colors vary from project to project, and personal preferences will certainly vary, too. For most of the pieces in this book, you can get by with the handful of basic colors listed below.

Basic supplies include a small assortment of acrylic craft paints, brushes, pencil, straightedge, marker and wood filler.

Fabric Paints. Fabric paint, which is a thicker version of acrylic and often applied straight from the bottle, offers an added element of texture since it stands out from the surface. I use it for delicate architectural details, for adding holiday trims or covering a roof with snow. I've also used fabric paint to decorate "everlasting" rock gingerbread houses.

Brushes

Most cottages can be painted with a maximum of three types of brushes, including one small, narrow brush used for fine lines and details. My choice for this is a Loew-Cornell script liner in a 0 or 1 size, but if you plan to concentrate on very small pieces, you might prefer a shorter bristle for better control. I don't believe in expensive brushes, but I'll pay four to five dollars for a detail brush that will hold a nice point.

A medium-sized tapered brush is handy for painting bushes and shrubs and for filling in doors and windows. A number 3 or 4 round brush from any craft supply store will do.

For larger areas, like coloring in rooftops or walls, try a round, tapered craft brush in a number 6 or 7, or a square-shaped brush in the same size.

Basic Colors:
- Black
- White
- Red
- Blue—medium shade; Dutch Blue or Cobalt
- Yellow
- Brown—either Burnt Sienna or Brown Oxide

Optional Colors:
- Metallic Silver (for "tin" barn roofs)
- Ochre
- Dark Green

Rock gingerbread houses make striking holiday centerpieces.

Wood Filler

A tube of 3-in-One brand Plastic Wood or Leech Real Wood Filler is needed for the projects in this book. Either of these products does a good job of hiding flaws, making chimneys and adding other small details to your pieces. This material dries quickly, is easy to paint over and is nearly as tough as rock. Personally I prefer Leech's product because it's somewhat easier to mold into shapes. A tube costing well under two dollars can be found at any hardware store. Occasionally with a new tube, the wood filler may come out runny at first. If so, wipe it off with a paper towel and squeeze out any excess until it comes out the consistency of peanut butter.

Either one of these brands of wood filler is perfect for adding details to rocks.

Miscellaneous

Other helpful items include a short straightedge ruler, pencils and fine-tipped felt markers (or laundry markers). A supply of old newspapers will come in handy to protect your painting surface from abrasion as well as providing a convenient place for test strokes and blotting excess paint or water from your brush.

Picture Collection

You may want to assemble a collection of pictures or photos of cottages and other buildings that appeal to you as a resource for ideas. While this book will supply many basic ideas for finishes like brick, stucco or stone, and architectural details such as window varieties, roof lines, dormers, porches and so on, thousands more styles and color combinations have been used on dwellings across the country. Victorian houses in particular, especially those sometimes called "Painted Ladies," offer a dizzying array of color combinations and details.

Pay attention also to the shrubs and flowers planted around houses that could be translated into striking finishing touches on your own miniature creations. Over time I've amassed a collection of photos and clippings that provide great ideas.

Let's Paint

Once you've picked up some promising rocks and gathered supplies, you're ready to begin. I've arranged the projects in this book roughly in order of difficulty so that beginning painters may gain skill and confidence as they work through them. More experienced painters may prefer to skip around.

If you mess up, please don't panic. Simply paint over the problem and try again. Or toss out that rock and try another. Adapt my instructions to your own tastes and skills, and never be afraid to experiment. There are as many ways to paint as there are people who want to, and this book is intended as an inspiration and guide to get you started.

The most important advice I can give is to have fun. Your work will benefit if you allow yourself to play.

A collection of photos such as this one will provide a wealth of painting ideas.

Painting Houses, Cottages and Towns on Rocks

How to Paint a
Basic Rock Cottage

You may feel ready at this point to plunge right in and try one of the more elaborate designs. If you are an experienced painter, whether on paper or canvas, or as a crafter on wood, china or other mediums, there is no reason not to start off with something more challenging if you wish. However, if you are just starting out, or if you haven't painted lately, this chapter is a good place to begin.

Study the house shapes below. They'll give you an idea of what to look for when you go rock-hunting for a basic cottage.

What You'll Need

- Acrylic paints in White, Yellow Ochre, Black, Burnt Sienna and Green
- Pencil
- Straightedge
- Tube of wood filler
- Assorted small and medium brushes
- Optional: a spray can of clear acrylic finish; blunt table knife

Rocks break in random ways and you're unlikely to find rocks exactly like any of the shapes at left. The stone I've selected for this project has several interesting imperfections. The roof line slants at a slightly skewed angle, and there's an odd bump along the front.

Look for simple house shapes like these to make a basic cottage.

Side view

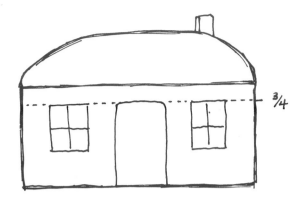

3/4

2nd STORY

1/2

1ST STORY

Make your door about three-fourths the height of the first storey.

1 Layout

Once you've selected a promising rock, turn it over and around to check out every angle. The front of your house should offer mostly flat surfaces that will be easy to paint on. At the very least, it should have flat places where the door and windows will go. Use a pencil to sketch in a front door. It can be centered or set to one side. (If needed, use a straightedge to determine the rock's center.) Since my rock has a bump near the center portion, I've decided to place my door in the middle. This way I can transform the uneven place in the foundation into a concealing shrub beside the door.

Beginners tend to oversize or undersize the doors. To keep the door in proper proportion, make it approximately three-fourths as tall as the first storey, excluding the roof. My cottage has only one storey, but if you choose to make two or more storeys, divide the walls evenly and sketch in guidelines to keep the upper windows even.

Window size is totally up to you. Smaller windows will make the cottage look more antique. Whatever the size, make sure the windows are evenly spaced and the same size. Use your straightedge to line up the tops with the top of the door and to ensure that the window bottoms are level.

Whether you paint windows on the sides and back is up to you. Most rock

cottages are designed to be viewed mainly from the front. If you elect to do windows on the sides, place them at the same height as the front windows. Now look over your layout. Once you're satisfied, you may want to go over your pencil lines with a pointed marker to help them stand out.

2 Add a Chimney

If you want to add a chimney, this is a good time to do it. Usually chimneys are placed at one end or the other, or in the center. I have placed my chimney slightly off center, however, to cover up a small hole in the rock.

Holding the tube of wood filler against the rock, gently squeeze a small glob onto the roof and let it rest a minute or so to lose its tackiness. With your fingers (you may want to wear a rubber glove or moisten your fingers to keep the filler from sticking to them), or with the blade of a knife, carefully mold the filler, pressing it into the roof for a firm bond. Then shape it so that it stands up, more or less square, about one-half inch or so.

Some wood filler products are looser than others and have a tendency to sag. If your chimney won't stay up, try holding the rock upside down for a few minutes so gravity keeps it straight as it sets. Allow the filler to cure for at least an hour before handling the rock.

Use your ruler to keep windows level.

Squeeze a blob of wood filler for a chimney.

Shape the chimney with your fingers.

3 Paint the Walls

Houses come in every color under the sun. The choice is completely up to you. Dark colors like slate blue, deep gray or burgundy are often seen in colonial style houses. Pastels like pink, aqua, pale yellow or blue are more Victorian in flavor. Farm houses are frequently white, while European cottages are likely to be buff, ochre or even brown.

To keep this first project simple, I've selected an off-white to suggest whitewashed stucco. To mix it, combine about half a teaspoon of white with a brushful of Yellow Ochre. Using a medium-sized brush, cover all the walls, leaving the doors and windows unpainted. Allow the paint to dry before going on.

Paint the walls with a flat brush.

4 Roof

Roof color also offers a variety of choices. Neutral colors like black, gray or brown are the most common, but there are plenty of white, red and green roofs around. Your choice should complement, not clash, with your wall color. I've decided on Burnt Sienna straight from the bottle. Use your larger brush to cover the roof quickly. Bring the roof color almost to the edge of the wall color without quite touching. Leave the chimney unpainted for now.

Paint the roof almost down to the wall color.

How to Paint a Basic Rock Cottage   17

5 Windows and Door

Window squares can be black, gray, a yellow-gold for the look of glowing lights, or perhaps blue, either pale or a darker shade. Use your smaller brush to fill in all the window squares.

While the windows are drying, add a bit of Burnt Sienna to a smaller amount of Yellow Ochre or white to get a soft brown. Use this color for the door.

Next, to make the features of your cottage stand out, frame them with a contrasting color. I've chosen white. Use your narrow brush for this step. First paint a band of trim between the roof and walls all around the house to create a tidy eave. Outline around the door and windows as well. It may be helpful to pick up your rock and hold it at different angles as you work.

Windows can look dark or lighted.

Fill in the door color.

White paint makes the eave stand out.

Outline the door and windows.

Painting Houses, Cottages and Towns on Rocks

Here are some sample door designs.

6 Chimney and Door Trim

For the chimney I've decided on a darker brown. Mix equal parts of Burnt Sienna and black to get a deep shade and carefully cover the entire chimney. Use this same dark brown to paint a thin line along the white window and door trim, as well as the trim at the eaves. This will make the white stand out. You could use a fine-tipped marker for the trim if it's more comfortable for you.

At this point you can paint in some vertical lines on the door to suggest boards if you wish. Add your doorknob at this time, too. There are numerous other door designs you can try, as shown in the sketches above.

Tilting the rock makes painting the door trim easier.

Here are some sample window designs.

7 Window Details

Windows, like doors, can be finished in a number of ways. Casement windows have a single horizontal line midway. Making a simple cross will give you four panes, or you may try a double cross for a more elaborate design if you are good at making straight, skinny lines. If you mess up, simply repaint and try again when it is dry.

A cross of white paint creates window panes, and vertical lines in a dark brown suggest boards on the door.

Painting Houses, Cottages and Towns on Rocks

Greenery adds a homey touch.

For shrubs, start with green, add black for shadows and light green for highlights.

8 Shrubs
Now mix green with a bit of black to get a darker green. Use a medium-sized round-tipped brush to dab in tapered shrub shapes along the foundation around the house. For a more realistic look, darken a bit of your green with black for a shadow at the bottom of the shrub. Lighten another small amount of green with a touch of yellow and white to highlight the shrub from above.

One straight vertical stroke creates shutters.

9 Shutters and Chimney
Using the same green, carefully stroke narrow rectangular shutters on both sides of each window. To make the shutters stand out, outline around them with black or darker green.

Detail the chimney by spacing some fine horizontal white lines from bottom to top. Intersperse short vertical lines for the look of brickwork.

Detail the chimney with white lines to resemble bricks.

Spray your rock cottage with clear acrylic finish to protect it.

10 Finishing Touches
Now look your cottage over from every angle. Are there any crooked lines to repaint and touch up? When you are satisfied, sign and date the bottom of the cottage with a felt pen or laundry marker. You may want to spray the piece with clear acrylic finish at this point to protect the paint and also heighten the colors.

How to Paint a Basic Rock Cottage

21

More Ideas . . .

To give you an idea of how versatile these rock cottages can be, I took the same rock and repainted it as a two-storey cottage (at right). By changing details, colors and landscaping, you can come up with endless variations. And, of course, no two rocks are ever quite the same to begin with.

The ink sketches on this page may give you some ideas for your own rock cottage. They range from a simple Cape Cod house to a thatched-roof cottage, from a two-storey saltbox to a neatly landscaped chateau.

These cozy cottages make great paperweights, conversation pieces or gifts. Several can form the nucleus of your own quaint village. Their simplicity has a folk art air that just might, in time, make them sought-after collector's items.

Here's a two-storey version of the same rock.

A two-storey saltbox.

A thatched-roof cottage.

A chateau.

A simple Cape Cod.

My mother painted this charming cottage.

Your cottage can even be decorated for the holidays. Add a dusting of snow if you wish.

Here is a group of "folksy" rock cottages.

How to Paint a Basic Rock Cottage

23

24   *Painting Houses, Cottages and Towns on Rocks*

How to Paint
A-Frames and Chalets

It may take a little practice to develop the knack for spotting some kinds of cottage rocks. There's nothing tricky, however, about this project. Triangle-shaped rocks are quite common, usually being points broken off larger rocks. Tall, narrow ones resemble A-frames, while shorter, wider ones look more like chalets. Keep in mind that you can work in a variety of sizes, from tiny to quite large.

Try to select a rock that has a more or less smooth front surface for easier painting. Also pay special attention to the bottom of the rock. It should be flat so the house will sit up straight. If you find a rock that seems to be a good choice but is a little tippy or perhaps has a chip along the base, such problems can be corrected by applying wood filler to the spot, smoothing it firmly in place and letting it dry.

Before doing any such repairs, make sure your rock is scrubbed clean and thoroughly dry.

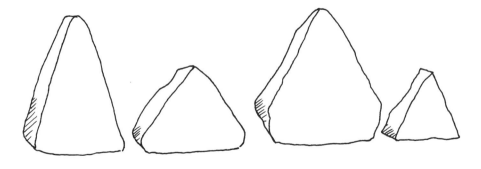

Here are some good rock shapes for painting an A-frame or chalet.

You won't find perfect rocks. Any of these will do very well.

For this project I've selected a rock that is approximately 4″ (10cm) tall and a little over 3″ (8cm) across the bottom.

1 Layout

A-frames and chalets often have a central front door with windows to either side, and a larger window or perhaps a balcony above. First measure the base and mark the halfway point. Then bisect the rock vertically. Next divide the height into thirds and center the door in the bottom third, using about three-fourths of that section's height. Align the window tops with the top of the door, leaving room for shutters. Hang the upper window from the top of the middle section. It can be a little larger since it is single. Add window boxes with sloping sides to complete the design.

When you're satisfied with your layout, select a site for the chimney. Squeeze wood filler onto the spot and let it sit a few minutes. Use a knife blade or your moistened fingers to gently shape it into a squared chimney. Allow it to dry and harden before going on.

Divide in half vertically.

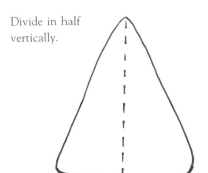

Divide in thirds horizontally.

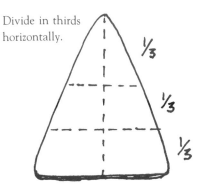

Center the door.

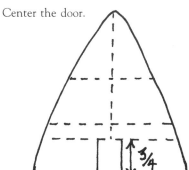

Align tops of windows.

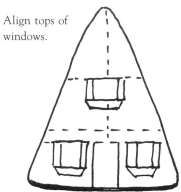

1. Divide the base in half and mark the center point.

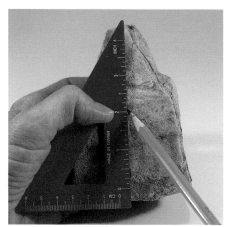

2. Bisect your rock vertically.

Shape a chimney with wood filler.

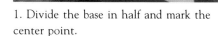

3. Divide it into thirds horizontally.

4. Draw in the door and windows.

2 Paint the Walls

The choice of colors is an individual one. For this house I've selected a cheery peach hue. Start with a small puddle each of red and yellow plus a larger amount of white. Add red and yellow in equal parts to the white paint until you get a peachy shade you like. Use a medium-sized brush to color in the front wall. Leave the windows, doors and a trace of your dividing guidelines uncovered. You may also paint the rear wall if you wish.

Paint the walls with a medium-sized brush.

Fill in the window squares.

3 Windows, Roof and Eaves

Switch to black paint and fill in the window squares and the upper half of the door. While these areas dry, mix a large puddle of red with enough black to get a deep brown. Cover both angles of the roof all the way to the base and right up to the edges of the front. To create a scalloped look along the eaves, use a small round bristle brush to dab paint at even intervals.

Color in the roof all the way to the base.

Press dabs of paint along the eaves to create a scalloped edge.

Do the trim design in
three simple steps.

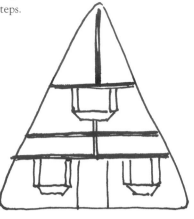

4 Decorative Trim
Switch to a smaller brush and use the same dark brown to create a decorative pattern of wooden cross pieces. Also fill in the bottom half of the door and outline around the upper half.

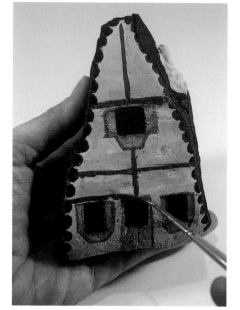

Use your narrow script liner brush to paint the wooden cross pieces.

Outline the door
and fill in the
bottom half.

Painting Houses, Cottages and Towns on Rocks

Mint green shutters complement the peach walls.

Practice on scrap paper before painting these fine windowpane lines.

Fill in the window boxes with white.

5 Window Details

To paint the shutters use your small round brush and mix medium green paint with enough white to soften it to a mint shade. Try to keep the edges straight.

Switch to white paint. For the windowpane lines you'll need your narrowest brush. Do some test strokes on paper to check your paint's consistency, as well as for practice. Paint that's too thick tends to break and glob, while too much water will make your lines transparent. If you are unsteady, make simple cross lines instead of trying for a multipane look. For the upper half of the door you may opt to paint them on the diagonal for variety. Remember to paint a white frame around your windows as well. Fill in the window boxes below each window and paint the chimney white, too.

White also serves as a basecoat for the chimney.

6 Detailing the Front

To set off the eaves, try adding a dot of white to each scallop. You can also highlight the door by using Burnt Sienna inside the dark brown outline and by adding X-shaped lines to the bottom portion.

Decorative dots on the eaves add charm.   Add a crosspiece to the door.

7 Roof and Chimney Details

The same Burnt Sienna can be used to add shingles to the roof. If you are steady-handed, try making neat rows of *U*-shaped lines, each row offset from the one below it. Or you may prefer a more random look by creating a series of single and double *U*-shapes.

Squeeze a little black paint onto your painting palette and use various combinations of Burnt Sienna and black to create diverse shades of rocks on the chimney.

For the shingles, paint either even rows of U's or a random pattern here and there.

Make the chimney stones of variable size and shape.

8 Finishing Touches

You may want to use a dark shade of brown to outline around the shutters and window boxes so that they stand out clearly. At this point I decided that my decorative wood trim needed a couple more lines as well.

Check your design at this point and fine-tune anything that needs changing.

First, paint dark green leaves. Next, dab on some medium blue flowers. Finally, add some light blue dabs for highlights.

9 Window Box

For the window box greenery, mix blue and yellow and then darken it with a trace of black; or you can use dark green paint. Dab in the leaves with the tip of your small brush. Let them dry, then switch to blue and create flowers by stippling in dots along the top of the greenery. Add white to the blue and make a few paler dots for contrast.

Now look over your work carefully. Pay particular attention to the windowpane lines. If they seem crooked, too thick or too thin, you can cover them with black paint and try again.

Make your window boxes bloom with stippled flowers. Just dab color lightly with the point of your brush.

When you're satisfied with your finished chalet, sign the bottom with a marker. Use clear acrylic finish spray to seal the surfaces and brighten the colors.

More Ideas . . .

There are many variations you can try. Since every rock is unique, simply changing color schemes can make a dramatic difference when added to your new shape. Both A-frames and chalets radiate Old World charm without requiring great skill to create.

This alpine chalet has a small side window as well as very large window gardens.

Here I've used the same design as the project in this chapter, but on a different, smaller rock, and with a more subdued color scheme.

Here's a sketch of an A-frame with a fancy wood balcony railing.

Naturally, you can paint any flower color you like in the window box. On this rustic chalet, I've left the bare rock face for the front to give an old, weathered look.

This is a rather large and fancy chalet—perhaps the summer home of an Austrian notable.

This simple A-frame is distinguished by fancy window treatment and a large second-floor window box.

Here's a well-kept rock A-frame with decorative white railing at the windows.

Here are some more ideas for you to work with. Your chalets can be as plain or as fanciful as you wish, just by varying the decorative trim and the colors.

Painting Houses, Cottages and Towns on Rocks

How to Paint
Gnome Homes

There are a lot of variations that will work as gnome homes. For a cozy, organic look, I like to use rocks with rounded edges. It's especially exciting to come across rounded rocks that have bumps or funny protuberances that suggest multilevels or extensions.

Look for an egg-shaped or rounded rock with a flat bottom. The taller it stands, the more room you'll have for details. Your gnome home can be any size, from a mere pebble on up, but avoid rocks that are less than an inch high.

For this gnome home, I've chosen a rock the size and shape of a baking potato, about five inches long and two and one-half inches high.

As always, scrub and rinse your rock and let it dry before going on with your painting.

What You'll Need

- Acrylic paints in Dutch Blue, Bright Yellow, Burnt Sienna, Black and White
- Pencil
- Assorted brushes
- Tube of wood filler
- Blunt tableknife

I chose this rock for my gnome home.

Here's a selection of good gnome home shapes.

This knobby rock was a real find. You'll probably want to try something simpler first.

Look what's peeking out from your flower bed!

35

1 Layout

The most important element of this design is the thatched roof that covers nearly half the rock. Using your eye or a straightedge, divide the rock in two horizontally, as shown in the sketch above.

The door can be placed on either side or in the center. Allow the door to stand slightly above the dividing line, as it will be tucked underneath the edge of the roof later on. Round off the top edge of the door.

Next place a square window to either side of the door. If your rock roof is round enough to allow room, sketch in a smaller square window to one side of the roof.

To indicate thatched dormers, sketch in a broad, slightly pointed half circle above the doorway, flanked by two somewhat smaller dormers over the two bottom windows. Make an even smaller dormer above the roof window. Finally, add windowsills to the bottoms of the two lower windows.

Before going on, form a chimney on the roof opposite the upper window. Squeeze out a small gob of wood filler, and shape it with your fingers or the blade of a knife. Let it dry for thirty minutes or longer before going on to the next step.

With your pencil, sketch your layout on the rock.

Squeeze out a tiny bit of wood filler for the chimney.

Press the wood filler into a chimney shape and let it dry.

Painting Houses, Cottages and Towns on Rocks

2 Paint the Walls

As with all the projects in this book, the choice of colors is yours. Gnome homes look best in soft colors: cream, pale blue, white or rose. I have chosen a very pale shade of blue using a mixture of Dutch Blue and lots of white.

Paint in the walls all the way around your rock, leaving the door and windows unpainted. Shade the wall just below the eaves, using the same blue-and-white mixture, with a touch more blue pigment added and just enough black to darken the color to a contrasting blue-gray. Shade below the windowsills as well.

3 Windows

Use black to fill in the window squares, leaving an unpainted border between the black and the blue wall color. Let the black paint dry thoroughly.

You can create round window panes by using a small blunt brush to dab in rows of bright yellow circles. These may need touching up with black later on to make them more uniform. Remember to do little yellow window panes in the upper window as well. Also paint a small yellow diamond-shaped window in the upper center of the door.

4 Door and Window Frames

Switch to white paint and carefully outline the two sides and bottom of each window. Fill in the door with white, and add a bottom step in white if there is room on your rock.

When the white is dry, use your script liner to outline the outside edges of your door and windows. (Don't forget the roof window.) Outline the diamond-shaped window in the door as well.

Paint the walls all the way around your rock.

Add depth with contrasting blue-gray shadows.

Darken the window squares with black paint.

Bright yellow windowpanes create a cozy glow.

Paint the door and window frames with white.

Carefully outline the edges in black.

5 Paint the Thatched Roof

Use a larger brush and bright yellow paint to paint in the roof. If needed, leave a trace of your pencil sketch uncovered to indicate the curved shape of the dormers. Allow your brushstrokes to encroach slightly into the shadowed portions of the walls. These downward strokes should be somewhat ragged to suggest the look of thatch.

Next, mix a few drops of Burnt Sienna into a small amount of yellow to get a reddish-gold shade. Using your script liner brush, make fine lines resembling hay on the roof. (Refer to the sketch at right for the direction your brush should take.)

When you have enough detail, mix Burnt Sienna with a little black to get a dark brown. Use this to outline the curved top of each dormer and to create feathery lines in the thatch along the bottom of the eaves.

Paint the roof color over the entire top of the rock.

Follow the directional arrows to paint the thatched roof with fine lines to resemble hay.

Fine lines in a darker shade indicate thatch.

Even darker lines emphasize contours.

Painting Houses, Cottages and Towns on Rocks

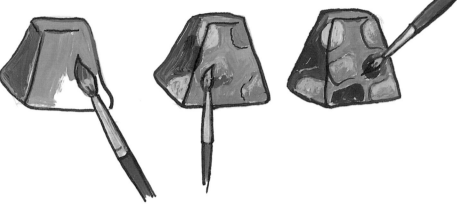

6 Add the Chimney

Paint the entire chimney pale gray and let it dry. Then create the look of large stones using a deeper shade of gray tinted with varying amounts of brown and blue.

Detail the chimney in three easy steps: 1) Paint the dried wood filler with pale gray, 2) dot in some light-colored stones, then 3) add darker-colored stones and some shading for dimension.

7 Finishing Touches

With your script liner and a little black paint, add a few board lines on the front door and a handle. Next, create a border of flowers by stroking in one short vertical green stem and a shorter leaf sprouting from each side. When the green is dry, go back and add a dot of bright color to the top of each stem.

Here's your completed gnome home. Look it over to make sure you're satisfied, then sign and seal it with clear acrylic finish.

How to Paint Gnome Homes

More Ideas . . .

Add Dimension to a Thatched Roof

For a more dramatic, three-dimensional look, use wood filler to emphasize the thatched roof contours.

1. Squeeze out some wood filler as if it were toothpaste, following your sketched-in eave lines.

2. Gently smooth the filler into the rock along the top edge, leaving the lower part standing out.

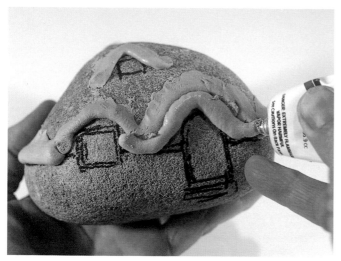

3. Add more wood filler if needed for volume.

4. Finally, use a knife blade to score the eaves along the top. This helps obscure the joint and adds to the "thatch" look.

5. Allow the wood filler to dry thoroughly before you begin to paint your rock.

Once the wood filler is painted, it has the depth and dimension of a real thatched roof.

Painting Houses, Cottages and Towns on Rocks

Place a few gnome homes in your garden or among the trees to attract small children or elves.

Try tucking them among your house plants.

These cottages are particularly attractive in small groupings. Varying the size, colors and details will allow you to come up with an endless array of cottages sure to set your imagination in flight.

How to Paint Gnome Homes

Painting Houses, Cottages and Towns on Rocks

How to Paint
Barns

These rustic buildings with their tin roofs, haylofts and cavernous doors are an integral part of our countryside. They are also cute and easy to paint.

Barns come in a variety of shapes from simple sheds to the classic gambrel roof version. As with other rock structures, it's unlikely that you'll come across an absolutely perfect barn-shaped rock. Instead, concentrate on looking for a rock that seems to suggest one of the classic shapes shown below.

Remember that unlike A-frames or chalets, barns should be deeper from front to back since they are designed as storage buildings.

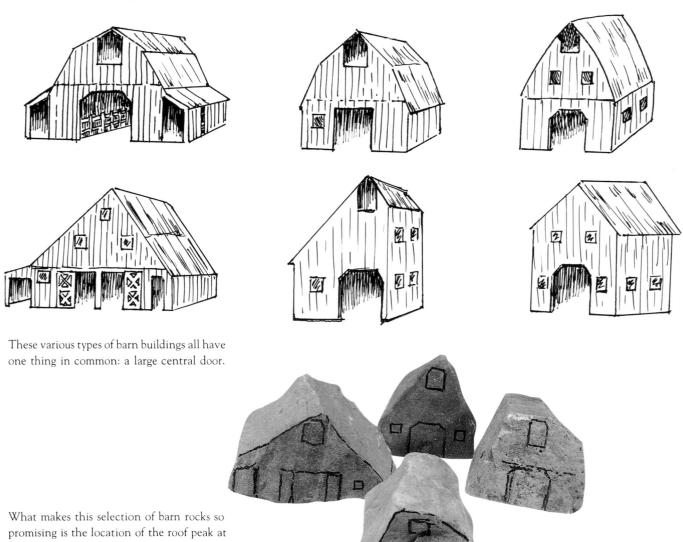

These various types of barn buildings all have one thing in common: a large central door.

What makes this selection of barn rocks so promising is the location of the roof peak at or near the center.

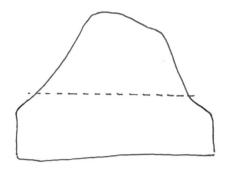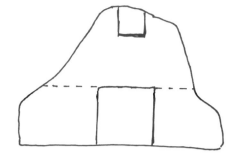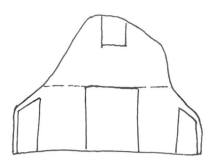

1 Layout

One of the reasons barns are so easy to create is that they have relatively few structural details. Usually there is a large central door, an upper loft opening and some combination of side doors and/or windows. You can customize these basic features by adding details like piles of hay, livestock, a tractor or even a farmer.

Start by sketching in the square main door. It should be approximately half as tall as the barn itself. The loft is a smaller, rectangular opening just below the top of the roof. For this project I'm adding side openings since the rock flares out to accommodate them. A row of stalls to one side can also add visual interest. If you opt to keep the sides plain you may want to darken a narrow space here and there to resemble missing boards.

If the sides where the roof ends are uneven, use your pencil to straighten them out. Later you can hide the unevenness with paint.

2 Paint the Openings

Fill in all openings with black paint. Don't forget the side stalls and any missing boards you sketched in.

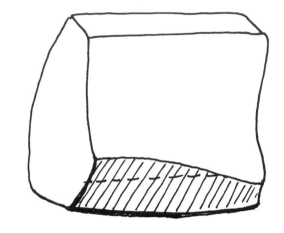

Disguise an uneven lower roofline by drawing a straight line with your pencil. Paint along this line later to visually even it out.

Paint all openings black.

3 Paint the Walls

Barns can be deep red, weathered gray or even white. For this project I've chosen to do a classic red barn. When the black paint is dry, mix equal parts of red and Burnt Sienna to get a rich, rusty red. Use your medium-sized brush to cover all the remaining wall areas.

Burnt Sienna and red combine for a perfect barn hue.

4 Roof

Rinse your brush thoroughly and let the walls dry. For the roof I like the look of shiny silver but you may opt to mix white with enough black to get a pale gray. Add some blue to give it a bluish cast. Cover the entire roof area and let it dry. If the edge of the roof slopes, remember to correct this by painting the bottom edge of the roof in a straight line parallel to the flat bottom.

Metallic silver makes a realistic-looking tin roof.

5 Roof Panels

Next mix red and black into a deep brown and use your script liner to define individual tin panels. Allow these lines to follow the natural contours of your rock.

Thin lines suggest tin panels.

6 Define Edges

Use the same dark brown to define the edges of the roof along the sides, front and back, and to bisect the front wall just above the main door.

Paint a brown line along the roof line and above the main door.

7 Door Frames

Rinse your brush and mix Burnt Sienna with a touch of black for a medium shade of brown, then lighten it up with a bit of white. Use this color to frame and set off the doors and loft. Leave a narrow line of black in place around the outsides of these frames.

Emphasize the openings with a touch of light brown.

Painting Houses, Cottages and Towns on Rocks

8 Rust

For the look of rusting tin, mix red with a small amount of Burnt Sienna and a trace of black. Use a medium brush to lightly feather this color on the tops and bottoms of the tin roof panels. For feathery strokes, gently splay your brush by pressing it on the palette until the hairs separate. Do more rust marks on some, less on others for a random look.

Feathery strokes with a splayed brush suggest a rusting roof.

9 Lumber Lines

Return to your narrow brush and dark brown or black paint. Take special care as you paint lumber lines on your barn walls. They can vary in width, but should be parallel to one another. If you mess up, simply repaint the barn color and try again.

Barn boards can vary in width, but should be parallel.

10 Weathered Look

If you'd like to give your barn a more rustic, weathered appearance, combine small amounts of red, Yellow Ochre and a trace of white. Feather this color onto some of your boards in a random manner.

Some lighter boards lend a weathered look to your barn.

11 Hay Loft

You can leave your barn plain and empty, but a loft full of golden hay makes for a welcome splash of color. Use your narrow brush with Ochre to create a pile of hay, then switch to yellow to highlight the top of the pile with random crosshatched lines. Blend a brushful of Burnt Sienna and Ochre together to shadow the very bottom of the pile.

Paint hay in the loft in three steps: First, paint the hay pile Ochre, then add yellow highlights on top, finally a few tan shadows at the bottom.

Some hay in the loft adds a splash of color.

12 Peek Inside

For the main opening I decided to have a horse peeking out over stable rails. You might prefer one of the other farm scenes shown below, or you can design your own.

The light goes partway into the barn door revealing what's just inside.

You can use one of these barn scenes, or design your own.

Painting Houses, Cottages and Towns on Rocks

More Ideas . . .

These barns can be displayed alone or teamed up with a farmhouse to create a cute vignette (see page 42). Barns can also add a quaint touch of country to your rock village.

The wide roofs make a perfect place to add billboard-type highway signs, or to personalize your barn as a gift.

Here's an idea for a barn with hay bales stacked inside.

Here's this chapter's barn (on the right) along with two others and a little shed. Roof billboards can show a familiar advertisement or can be personalized with your family name, or the name of the recipient.

Painting Houses, Cottages and Towns on Rocks

How to Paint a
Country Church

(or a Little Red Schoolhouse)

The American landscape would hardly be complete without this historic symbol of enduring faith, the country church. Along with one-room schoolhouses, these buildings were the very heart of countless rural communities.

To create either the church or the schoolhouse, look for rocks that, in addition to the requisite flat bottom, also offer sloping roof angles and a flat front side. It's helpful if the side walls are square and somewhat flat, but mi-

nor imperfections can be concealed with shrubbery.

Occasionally I come across "church rocks" that actually feature steeple-like protuberances. That's certainly a plus, but a steeple can always be built up out of wood filler.

Your church or schoolhouse may be any size, but if you are creating a village, look for rocks that fall within the general scale of the buildings you've already done.

What You'll Need

- Acrylic paints in White, Blue, Black, Yellow, Brown, Red and Green (optional)
- Pencil
- Straightedge
- Assorted brushes
- Tube of wood filler
- Optional: fine-tipped black marker

A wide range of rock shapes will work as churches or schools.

   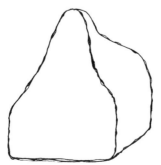

1 Preparing Your Rock

Although I've found more nearly perfect church rocks, I've chosen a rather average one to demonstrate this project. It has a number of flaws, but size-wise it fits with the pieces I've already painted. One of the rock's draw-backs is that it is not symmetrical; the rooflines don't quite match each other. Also, the right side wall curves out. In spite of these defects, it will still make a fine church. As always, scrub and rinse your rock before beginning.

Since the steeple is one of the most defining elements of either church or schoolhouse, it's the first thing you'll want to establish. As with chimneys, squeeze a good-sized gob of wood filler onto the steeple site. For a church, this would be right at the top of the roof in front. For schools, place it squarely in the middle of the roof. Allow the wood filler to set up for a minute or so before gently shaping it into a square, making sure it adheres smoothly and firmly to the rock. Since a steeple is larger than most chimneys, it's advisable to create a secure base first, let it dry, then add an upper portion. Lightly pinch the wood filler to create an angled or pointed steeple.

Is there any place on your rock that could use touching up? On mine I added a line of putty along the roofline on the right side to minimize the asymmetry of the roof angles. I then smoothed and blended it into the rock surface, allowing it to harden before going on to the next step.

Use plenty of wood filler for a steeple.

Let the wood filler set up for a minute, then gently pinch to shape.

A line of wood filler along the roofline on one side adds symmetry.

Painting Houses, Cottages and Towns on Rocks

2 Layout

As with all buildings, churches offer a number of choices. The size, color and number of windows are all up to you. This design, with a central double door, half-round windows and a bell set into the steeple, captures the tranquil simplicity of a classic country church. For a school, modify the same basic design, making the doors and windows rectangular instead.

If you are adding to a village, remember to keep the door height consistent with your other buildings, and leave room below for a couple of steps. The tops of the flanking windows should be set on a line even with the top of the door. Place one, two or more matching windows on the sides of the building, depending on how much room there is on your rock. These windows should be at the same height as your front windows. Sketch in the edges of the roof along the sides, the front and the back. Use a ruler if needed to ensure the front corners of the roof match.

Make sure the windows are all at the same height.

3 Paint the Walls

Begin painting by using white to cover the walls, working around the door and windows. Paint the sides of the steeple white for now. If you're painting a school, substitute bright red for the walls.

Cover the walls with white.

4 Roof

The roof can be any color, but a somber shade of blue, green, brown or gray is most appropriate. For this project I mixed medium blue with enough black to get a deep navy blue. Carefully color in the steeple roof, then move down to paint the main roof. Keep the eave lines as straight as you can, both along the sides and in front where they slope up towards the steeple.

Paint the roof, including the top of the steeple.

5 Outlines

Switch to your narrowest brush and black paint to outline the doors, windows and the front steps.

Outline all the openings.

Draw horizontal lines to indicate front steps.

Painting Houses, Cottages and Towns on Rocks

Here are three simple steps for a bell shape: First, paint an oval of white; second, paint another oval of white; third, connect the two ovals.

6 Steeple Detail

Fill in the front steeple opening, leaving a small bell shape unpainted. Repeat on all sides of the steeple.

Paint black around the bell shape.

Don't forget to outline the windows on the sides of your church, too.

7 Front Steps

Now add a touch of white to make a soft gray and shade the risers of your front steps.

Shadow the front steps with gray.

Yellow paint makes your bell stand out.

8 Bell

Clean your brush and switch to bright yellow paint. Fill in the bell shape on all three sides of the steeple.

How to Paint a Country Church

9 Stained Glass

Use the same yellow to color in the upper portions of all your stained glass windows (or feel free to come up with your own glass design if you prefer). Add red to the yellow to get a warm orange. Blend this orange into the center of the windows below the yellow. Complete the window color by painting in a touch of blue at the bottom, then add yellow to the blue to get green and blend it upward into the orange. When the windows have dried, switch to black paint and create a design that looks like leaded panes.

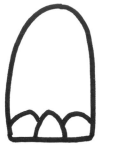  

Simple curved black lines look like lead dividers.

10 Bell Detail

To detail the bell, use a tiny bit of your orange paint. Outline the bell, and shade the inside.

Add color for stained glass windows.

When the color dries, draw a pattern with black paint to resemble lead dividers.

Add an orange line to show the flare of the bell.

11 More Details

Fill in the door with dark brown paint. When it dries, go around the doorway with black, if needed, to make it stand out, and add a dividing line down the center. Outline around the eaves and delineate the corners of the front walls as well.

Paint the front door with dark brown, then outline the doorway with black.

Clarify the edges by outlining the roof and sides with black.

12 Add Greenery

Because my right side wall bows out, I placed a large evergreen shrub at the front corner to conceal the problem. Another bush below one window and lush grass below the other breaks up the symmetry. Paint the bush shape with dark green first, then add strokes of yellow green for detail and highlights.

Greenery softens the edges and conceals flaws. Paint the landscaping freely—add some flowers if you want.

13 Finishing Touches

Detail the roof by creating a shingled look. Mix up a much paler shade of your roof color by adding white to it. Use it to make rows of L-shaped shingles with your narrow script liner brush. On the other side of the roof reverse your *L*-shapes.

You can stop at this point, or, if you have a steady hand, you may go on to add lines of pale blue clapboard siding to the front and sides. Remember you can always paint over any uneven lines and redo them if necessary.

To make the door stand out against the siding lines, add a frame of white around it and outline it with blue-gray.

Simple *L*-shaped shingles accent the roof.

Clapboard siding adds a realistic country touch.

Accentuate the doorway with an arched white frame outlined in blue-gray.

Here's the finished church in a country setting.

More Ideas . . .

You may want to make a sign above the door to personalize your church. Other decorative options above the door include a simple cross or perhaps another stained glass window.

One charming variation is to add a snow-covered roof, with delicate drifts of white among the branches of greenery.

Churches and schoolhouses make particularly appropriate and welcome gifts for pastors or teachers.

A sign above the door adds a personal touch. Paint an arch with white paint and write your church's name with a marker.

Create a snow setting for your rock church, complete with snow-dusted rock "evergreens."

Here are the rocks you saw on page 51 painted as country churches and little red schoolhouses.

Painting Houses, Cottages and Towns on Rocks

How to Paint
Small Town Shops

Small businesses are a vital element of any community, and you'll certainly want to add some to your growing village. Shop buildings are so simple, and the rock shapes for them so common, that you might end up painting an entire village main street!

Like the other projects in this book, commercial buildings come in a number of sizes and shapes. In fact, you will add realism by selecting rocks in a variety of heights and widths.

Almost any squarish or rectangular rock will work as a shop. The most important features are a relatively flat front wall, straight sides, and, of course, a flat bottom. A rock that tilts forward or backward but is otherwise suitable can be doctored by adding a line of wood filler to the bottom along the front or rear side to make it sit up straight. Wood filler can also even out distracting gaps along the bottom of the front wall. The roof may be flat, slanted like a shed-type roof, or have a combination of angles. The back side is unimportant since it's rarely seen.

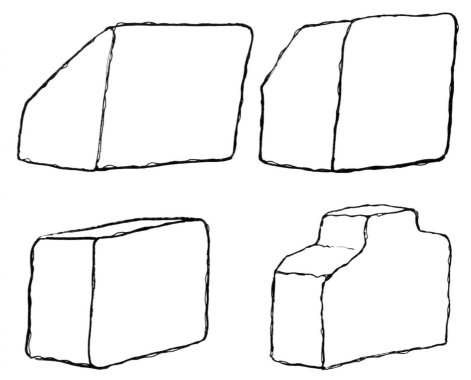

Here are four good rock shapes for main street shops.

What You'll Need

- Acrylic paints in Burnt Sienna, White, Yellow Ochre, Black, Red and Blue
- Pencil or fine-tipped marker
- Straightedge
- Tube of wood filler
- Assorted brushes

The rock I've chosen has a large flat front and good straight side walls. In fact, its only flaw is a slight nick in the lower right corner, so minor I'm not even going to patch it.

1 Layout

Once a rock is selected and scrubbed, use a pencil or marker to lay out the simple design. All store buildings have several elements in common: large display windows, a central or offset door and place for signage. Taller rocks look great with windows along the upper storey as well. The door may be set between two windows, or placed to one side with a prominent flanking display window. Keep it simple at this stage, just drawing the basic shapes of the door, windows and sign.

How you choose to make the sign depends on how comfortable you are with lettering. It takes more skill and a steadier hand to letter across a skinny sign than a wide one.

Once you've decided on a design, use a straightedge to help line up the door and window tops. Remember that door size should roughly match those of your other buildings if you are working on a whole village.

Here are several layout alternatives. The signage helps make each store front unique.

Painting Houses, Cottages and Towns on Rocks

2 Cover the Surface

If you're planning to paint more than one store, each should have a unique look. One striking choice is to leave the rock surface unpainted and use a darker or lighter color to paint in brick-and-mortar lines. The dry goods building on page 66 illustrates this option. This can be especially attractive when your stone is either quite dark or very light. However, the rock I've selected is medium gray, allowing neither dark nor light mortar lines to stand out. Instead, I've decided to paint it a warm brown color. To mix this color, combine equal parts of Burnt Sienna and white. Use a medium-sized brush to cover the front wall of your building, leaving the door, windows and sign space unpainted for now. Cover the sides of your store, and the rear wall if you wish. Switch to black paint for filling in the door and window glass.

3 Roof

The roof should be darker or lighter than your walls. I've chosen to go darker, adding black and a bit more Burnt Sienna to my wall color for a deep milk chocolate color that makes a subtle but pleasing contrast.

Paint the basecoat, covering the front wall, sides and back if desired.

Blacken the door and window openings.

A contrasting color sets off the roof; it should be either lighter or darker than the front.

4 Sign Color

Now choose a base color for your sign. Light colors like white or yellow allow dark lettering to show up clearly. A dark red, blue or green base can be attractive with light-colored letters. If you feel more comfortable lettering with a marker, use a light-colored base. Here I'm using pure white.

Fill in the sign space with a light color if you are going to use a marker for lettering.

5 Outline the Edges

Mix Yellow Ochre with white to get a soft golden yellow. Use a script liner or other narrow brush to carefully outline all the windows. You may add a line across the middle to create a double-hung window, or make windowpanes. Frame in the doorway as well, filling in the bottom portion to form a kickplate.

While you have this color on your brush, add decorative rectangles below each display window.

Rinse out your brush and use straight Burnt Sienna to outline around the sign space and along the top and side corners of the building. Fill in the centers of the rectangles below the display windows as well.

Framing doors and windows helps define them.

Decorative trim adds visual interest.

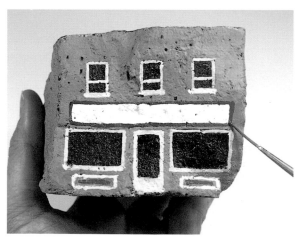

Outline around the sign and the edges of the building to create depth and dimension.

Painting Houses, Cottages and Towns on Rocks

6 Sign Lettering

To help space your sign letters correctly, practice first on paper. Measure out the same sized area as the sign on your rock store and use a pencil to practice your lettering. When you're satisfied, place your practice sign below the sign space and copy it, using a Sharpie or other fine-tipped permanent marker. The sharper the point, the more detailed your letters can be. If you mess up, just repaint the sign space and try again after it dries. I decided to add some definition by outlining the windows with the marker, too.

Practice your sign lettering on paper first. Be sure to leave enough white space around the letters so the sign doesn't look crowded.

If you want, outline around light areas with your marker.

7 Finishing Touches

For more detail, I placed white banners in the upper portion of each display window for more signage, and hung an "open" sign in the door. Simple curtains in bluish-white paint soften the upper-storey windows, and a few narrow diagonal lines add the sheen of glass to the windows.

I decided my store needed a bit more zip, so I added a broken line of soft gold, resembling a row of decorative bricks, across the top.

Add curtains to your windows with bluish-white paint. Diagonal streaks of gray and white will create the illusion of reflecting glass.

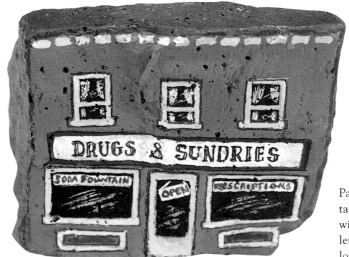

Paint some curtains in the upper windows, and red-lettered signs in the lower ones.

More Ideas . . .

There are numerous variations to this basic design. While small businesses and shops are right at home as part of a village scene, they can also be customized as gifts for family and friends who own their own businesses. Study the details of the "real" storefront and copy the signage as carefully as you can for an authentic look.

This general store is painted on a rock with a squarish extension on top.

Here's a row of shops that work together as a small town main street. Notice how the doors and windows are in proportion to each other.

Paint an appropriate display of merchandise in the windows for added interest.

I used the look of red bricks for this bakery.

Gray paint and a contrasting wainscot give my barber shop its unique look.

I've personalized this small bookstore in honor of my publisher.

Tall narrow rocks like this make good downtown stores built in the early part of this century.

Painting Houses, Cottages and Towns on Rocks

How to Paint a
Produce Market

A welcome addition to any village, this perky produce market features a colorful awning and outside bins of fruits and veggies. To create it I selected a shorter rock than the one for the two-storeyed drugstore of the previous chapter.

Otherwise, the rock is similar. It has squared corners, a flat front and straight side walls. My rock's top is slightly uneven, but not enough to detract from the finished piece. Once you've selected your rock, scrub it and let it dry before going on.

What You'll Need

- Acrylic paints in Red, Yellow, Black, White, Ochre, Burnt Sienna, Blue and Green (optional)
- Pencil or marker
- Straightedge
- Assorted brushes

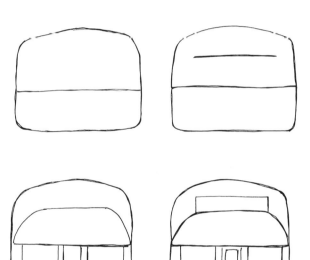

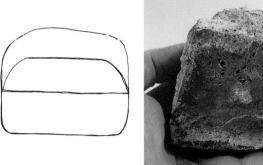

For a produce market, select a "one-storey" rock with a fairly flat front.

1 Layout

The layout for this piece is simple. Start by dividing your rock in two horizontally. This midline serves as the bottom edge of the awning. Next, center another straight, slightly shorter line just below the top of the rock, leaving room above it for sign space. Now connect the upper and lower lines by sketching a curving line at either end.

Place the door directly under the awning in the center. Add large rectangular windows that flank the door and sign space above the awning.

Use a marker to draw your basic layout following the sketches shown above.

2 Awning

First, use a medium-sized brush and black paint to fill in the windows and the center portion of the door. Then, with a pencil, divide the awning into seven equal portions that are narrow at the top and wider at the bottom. Begin with the one in the center, then curve the rest out, echoing the curved outside edges of the awning.

When you finish your guidelines, start at one end and color in every other stripe with red. Rinse your brush and color in the remaining sections with bright yellow.

Change to a narrower brush and use the yellow to outline the frames around the two display windows.

Paint the windows and door black.

Sketch in the awning stripes with pencil first.

Paint the red stripes starting with the outside.

Let the red paint dry a little before painting the yellow stripes.

Bright edges make the windows stand out.

Painting Houses, Cottages and Towns on Rocks

3 White Details

Switch to white paint to outline around the door next. Continue using white and detail the sides of the building with a chunky block pattern. Do this by painting horizontal, evenly spaced lines, then dividing each pair of lines into segments. Stagger the vertical dividing lines so they don't align with the ones above or below. Leave your sign space open for now.

Make one last row of blocks around the top edge of your rock. Then fill in the top of the roof with white.

Return now to the front of your store. Bring the lines of blocks around until they touch the edges of the display windows, the sides of the awning and the ends of the sign space. Fill in the sign space above the awning with white.

White paint defines the door.

The rock's natural texture creates a true "stone wall" between your mortar lines.

Make a final row of blocks at the top.

Paint the very top with white.

Now fill in the space reserved for your sign with white.

A

B

C

D

E

4 Fruit Barrels

Once all the structural elements are in place, it's time to begin adding the details that give this piece much of its appeal. The open barrels and bins full of fresh fruits and veggies can be done a couple of ways. You can make one large display unit as shown at far right, or follow the steps above to paint some produce in barrels and crates.

(A) Use Ochre softened with white to outline the barrels.

(B) Add a touch of Burnt Sienna and shade both the round top and the staves. For the crate, start with a drop of yellow and a dab of red to get orange, then soften it with Ochre so that it complements, yet subtly contrasts with, the barrels.

(C) Darken between the slats with a combination of black and Burnt Sienna.

(D) Mix a bright orange for the pile

of oranges, and bright red darkened slightly with black for your apples. Fill the center crate with unhusked corn, in three rows of long green ovals.

(E) Add yellow to the green and highlight the tops of the ovals. Finally, with the tip of your script liner and dark brown paint, outline around the oranges, apples and the corn to help them stand out. I added a tiny dot of white to each apple as a gleam, and a dab of yellow to the center of each orange.

Here's an alternate design for a fruit and vegetable display.

F

G

H

5 Melons

A heap of watermelons on the other side of the market helps balance the composition.

(F) Begin by painting a bottom row of four round or slightly oval melons in

a deep green shade. Add two or three melons to the second row.

(G) Mix enough white into your green to get a very light shade, and use the tip of your brush to dab this color in curved, crooked and broken lines

across your melons.

(H) To finish, switch to black and outline each melon and shade in the areas between and below each one.

Painting Houses, Cottages and Towns on Rocks

Here's how I painted the fruit and vegetable displays on my rock, using the basic steps shown at left.

1. Paint the round barrel.

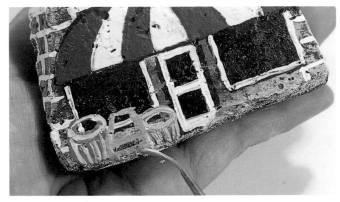

2. Add the crate.

3. Paint dark green ovals for watermelons.

4. Dot in some oranges.

5. Add green ears of corn.

6. Red dots make apples.

7. Highlight the apples.

8. Detail the watermelons.

How to Paint a Produce Market

6 Lettering the Sign

To prepare for lettering your sign, outline the edges of the signboard in black so that it stands out crisply. Use a pencil to sketch in your lettering. Simple capital letters are easiest. If you have trouble with spacing, simply re-paint the signboard and try again. When you're satisfied, use your script liner to paint over your sketched letters. Or you may be more comfortable lettering with a fine point felt-tipped marker (I use a laundry marker). This is also a good time to look over your produce market for other areas that need touching up. Outlining the sections of the awning will help define them.

After outlining the signboard in black, carefully pencil in your sign lettering.

Paint over your letters with black, or use a fine marker.

Use your script liner with black to make the colors of the awning stand out.

Painting Houses, Cottages and Towns on Rocks

7 Finishing Touches

A couple of price signs in the windows are a nice touch. I painted a yellow square at an angle on one side, and a white rectangle on the other side, with a rough suggestion of lettering on each. Then, to make the window glass appear shiny and reflective, I added a few diagonal streaks of pale blue-gray to each side. That completes this fetching little produce market.

Signs in the windows and glare on the glass add a realistic touch.

The Jones Market is now set up and ready for business.

Consider adding a customer looking at some of the produce as I've done on this market.

How to Paint a Produce Market

Painting Houses, Cottages and Towns on Rocks

How to Paint a
Farmhouse

An inviting front porch, dormer windows and charming simplicity are all earmarks of the classic farmhouse. But these quintessentially American structures are just as likely to be found lining the streets of older neighborhoods as they are to be paired off with barns in the midst of rural fields.

Many different rock shapes can be used to capture the "down home" look of an American farmhouse. Just driving through older working-class neighborhoods and noting the architectural details of the houses can be a great source of inspiration. You might even want to collect photos of farmhouses that appeal to you. These exercises will help in spotting the potential in a variety of rock shapes.

What You'll Need

- Acrylic paints in Yellow, White, Black, Green (or Blue) and Red
- Tube of wood filler
- Assorted brushes
- Pencil or marker
- Tableknife (optional)

Here is an assortment of farmhouse rocks before and after laying out the design. Notice where I've added some wood filler to enhance the shapes. See page 87 for finished examples of these rocks.

The rock I've chosen for this project is a rather plain one. You may prefer to look for one whose contours suggest more complex roof angles or other features that spark your imagination.

1 Preparation

Once you've selected a rock for this project, make sure that it's clean and dry. With wood filler, form a chimney to one side. Use your fingers or a tableknife blade to shape the material as it dries. Add a strip of wood filler along the line where the front porch roof will overhang. This is optional, but it will add depth to the porch. On my rock the front face is irregular, and an overhang will help minimize this. Smooth and blend the wood filler into the rock along the top so that it is firmly secured and appears to be part of the surface. To ensure the overhang is straight, you may want to sketch in a guideline first.

For the dormer window, squeeze a small glob of wood filler onto the roof in the center front, then use your fingers to pinch a flat front and peaked roof. A knife blade is helpful in getting sharper edges. If your dormer is large, try tilting the rock as it dries to keep the filler from sagging. Although I'm adding only one dormer window, you may elect to do two or even three. Let each addition harden before starting another to keep from damaging them.

Use wood filler to add architectural interest to your rock by forming a chimney, porch overhang and dormer.

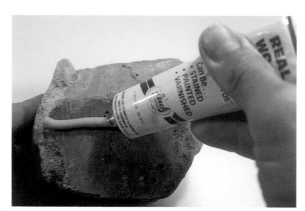

A thick line of wood filler forms a porch overhang.

Smooth and blend the wood filler into the rock's surface.

Press a peaked dormer into place.

2 Layout

When all your additions are thoroughly dry, sketch in your general layout. If you aren't sure what design you want, try making some sketches on paper. For this project, mark off the bottom third of the rock as the porch. Four porch posts should suffice. Start with one at either end, then evenly space the inside posts between the outside ones. Porch posts can be plain or set on pedestals of rock or brick. Place two or three steps between the two middle posts. Center the front door between them as well, starting at the top step.

Remember to keep your door size consistent with the doors of your other buildings if you want them to match. Now set a window between the posts on both sides of the door. The tops of the windows should be level with the top of the door. Place a window in your dormer, too. You may also want to sketch in windows on the sides of your house if there is room, and around back if you'd like. I kept my windows rather small so there would be enough space for shutters.

If you've used a pencil, you might want to go over your lines with a felt marker.

Wait until the wood filler hardens to draw your layout with a marker.

How to Paint a Farmhouse

79

3 Paint the Windows

Because I want my farmhouse to have a warm and welcoming look, I begin by painting the window openings yellow for a golden glow. If your yellow paint is on the pale or lemony side, add a touch of Ochre to deepen it. Fill in all the window squares, including the dormer and side windows. I also made a window in the upper portion of my front door.

Yellow paint gives windows a welcoming glow.

4 Paint the Walls

Switch to white paint to cover the walls. Remember to paint the siding around the dormer window, and on both sides of the house, ending with an inverted V-shape at the top of the roof.

To heighten the illusion of depth, add a touch of black to your white paint to get a medium gray. Use this color to darken the wall just below the porch overhang so that it appears to be shadowed by the roof. Color in the steps with this gray as well.

Paint the walls white on all sides of your rock. Don't forget the dormer.

Create a shadow under the porch overhang with gray.

Paint the steps gray, too.

5 Paint the Roof

Now mix your roof color. I chose a deep green. If you don't have this shade of green on hand you may darken a medium green with black, or combine blue and a little less yellow, then add black. Since there are no details, it's faster if you use a bigger brush for the roof. Leave a narrow space unpainted between the roof color and the walls.

With a large brush, paint the entire roof, including the dormer roof.

6 Brickwork

For the bricks of the chimney and porch, mix small amounts of red and yellow, then add a touch of white to get a soft reddish-orange. Use this color to cover the chimney, then fill in the porch foundation walls and porch post pedestals. Let the outlines for them remain uncovered for now.

Paint the brick areas of the porch a reddish-orange, but leave the posts alone for now.

7 White Details

When the roof paint has dried, delineate the eaves, using a script liner and white paint. While you're using white paint, color in the porch posts and highlight the top of each stair step, too. Now all bare rock should be covered except for the window shutters and front door.

Paint a white strip along the eaves to look like a rain gutter.

Now fill in the porch posts with white. Try not to paint over the outlines. But if you do, simply repaint them with black when the white dries.

Make a very thin line at the top of each step for a highlight.

Painting Houses, Cottages and Towns on Rocks

8 Black Details

Using your clean script liner or narrowest brush, switch to black paint. Go over your porch outlines to help them stand out. Next create a brick pattern by stroking a series of straight, narrow horizontal lines across the two wall sections, then breaking the lines into brick-sized segments, staggering the joints. Do the same thing on the pedestals. These horizontal lines need not match up with the ones on the wall sections, and will look better if they don't quite match. Don't forget to brick in the chimney, too.

Continuing with black details, outline the eave above your dormer, the window squares and porch posts. A simple cross in the windows will indicate panes.

Look over your piece to see if there are any other places that could use more emphasis. The corners of the house may require outlining, particularly if the edges are not straight or plumb.

Use the tip of your narrowest brush for very fine brick lines on the porch wall and chimney.

Emphasize important features with black outlines, and divide the windowpanes.

How to Paint a Farmhouse

83

9 Clapboard Siding

Mix up a pale gray and use it to paint clapboard siding along the wall areas. Remember you can always paint over any crooked lines and try again. If your gray paint is not light enough to contrast with the shadowed area below the porch overhang, lighten it so this area will also have the look of siding.

10 Shutters

To paint the window shutters and the roof shingles, mix up the same green color you used for the roof, then lighten it with enough white to get a clear contrast. Carefully fill in all the window shutters. You may need to go back later and outline your shutters with black if you paint over your previous outlines.

11 Shingles

For the roof shingles try using the tip of your script liner or the side of a shorter thin brush. Make a straight row of small, lighter green marks near the bottom of the porch overhang. Do a second row slightly above the first, with each mark set between the bottom row. Stagger subsequent rows of marks, working your way up to the peak of the roof. On the little dormer roof make the lines go sideways to echo the peak of the dormer. Turn your rock and detail the backside of the roof in the same manner.

Use your narrow brush to delineate clapboard siding.

In the shadow area of the clapboards, switch to light gray or white for contrast.

Shutters set off the windows. Choose a shutter color that harmonizes with your wall and roof colors.

This shingle pattern is decorative without being difficult.

12 Add Shrubs

Looking over my farmhouse at this point, I determined that the bottom front corners curved inward in a distracting way. To hide this, I decided to add wood filler to both corners to fill in the curves. Squeezing out a blob of filler with a fat bottom and allowing it to taper up, I created the shape of an evergreen shrub.

While my shrubs set up, I painted the front door. To get this deep brown, mix a drop of red with an even smaller drop of black.

When the shrubs dried, I painted them deep green, then added lighter, yellow-green highlights to the upper and middle portions. I also used the lighter green to feather in some fine lines as grass along the bottom of the porch walls.

Shrubs made from wood filler camouflage imperfect corners.

While the wood-filler shrubs dry, paint the door a deeper brown.

Paint a shrub in three easy steps: First, green. Next, black shadows at the bottom and finally, yellow-green highlights over the top.

Stroke some lighter green over dark green to paint your newly sculpted shrubs.

A few strokes of light green for grass along the bottom edge completes a basic farmhouse.

More Ideas . . .

Among the many variations you may want to try are: a silvery tin roof, wooden shake roof, or shingles in other colors, including burgundy, gray or black.

Farmhouse walls can also be painted in other color combinations. Porches may be surrounded by wooden railings or curlicued wrought iron instead of brick. With so many choices, you can create dozens of these quaint old farmhouses and give each and every one a distinct personality.

Here's a similar farmhouse with an interesting irregular roof.

This odd-shaped rock worked well as a farmhouse with a tin roof.

Here's a rambling, multigabled farmhouse for a large family. You can just imagine all the rooms inside.

These are the rocks you saw on page 77 with layouts only. Now they're ready to be placed in a village, or with a barn in a country setting.

How to Paint a Farmhouse

Painting Houses, Cottages and Towns on Rocks

How to Paint a
Colonial-Style Building

Classic Colonial, Greek Revival and Southern Colonial are three distinct examples of colonial-style buildings, all based to some degree on ancient Greek architecture. The primary element they share is a set of broad columns.

Greek Revival most resembles an ancient temple, with columns across the entire front and even along the sides. Southern Colonial usually features a sloping, less formal roofline. Classic Colonial confines its columns to an entryway, leaving the wings comparatively unadorned.

Between these three acknowledged types there are many variations. Fortunately for rock painters, the colonial building, in its many forms, makes an ideal project. It requires a basic square or rectangular rock that is common and easy to spot. And the impressive-looking details are surprisingly simple to paint. This style is equally suitable for residential or public structures, and is particularly appropriate for a courthouse or library, both nice additions to a village.

<table>
<tr><td colspan="2">What You'll Need</td></tr>
<tr><td>•</td><td>Acrylic paints in Black, White and Green</td></tr>
<tr><td>•</td><td>Pencil or fine-tipped marker</td></tr>
<tr><td>•</td><td>Tube of wood filler</td></tr>
<tr><td>•</td><td>Assorted brushes</td></tr>
</table>

Rocks for this project are relatively easy to find.

I'm going to use a long rectangular rock with a few flaws, but see how nice and flat the bottom is?

A bit of wood filler corrects the jagged edge along the top of my rock.

1 Preparation

I've chosen a rock with some flaws to show how easily minor imperfections can be overcome. My rock has an uneven top and a small notch right where I want to place the triangular front piece called a tympanum. I used a small amount of wood filler to fill in the notch and to bridge the different levels of the roof, downplaying them. You could use even more filler, if you wish, and shape the entire tympanum area of your rock or create a broad peaked angle at the roof.

If the rock you've chosen has a slanting roof, you can build up this triangle in order to achieve a classic look or just make the row of columns without it. A line of wood filler along the foundation will also be needed if you decide to build up wood-filler columns later (see page 95).

To the right are three of the rocks from the previous page. I want you to see the variety of ways to use the wood filler to enhance "colonial" rocks because your rock will not look just like mine.

On this rock I added a triangular front piece to a sloped roof.

This rock looks like a public building to me. I just enhanced its natural peak with wood filler.

This rock is a wonderful, long rectangle that just needed some wood-filler additions.

Painting Houses, Cottages and Towns on Rocks

2 Layout

Once you've made your wood-filler additions and allowed them to dry, sketch in your layout, using the sample sketches above to help with your design. Square rocks are more suited to the Revival style, while rectangular ones have room for wings at either side. A picture of the White House inspired my design.

The shape of the rock itself should suggest where the roofline should be. I sketched in a second line below the roofline to form a wide band across the front, then outlined a long, low tympanum. Use a pencil to rough in your initial lines, then go back over them with a marker when you're ready to paint.

By centering the door, I established where the inside columns would go, then added an outside set. There was ample room above the door for some kind of decoration so I opted for a fan-shaped window directly above the door and an octagonal window in the wall over it. I wasn't sure if I wanted two windows or four on each wing, so I decided to wait and just begin painting.

3 Paint the Roof

The fact that my roof was uneven helped me decide on a dark color that would minimize the irregularity. I used straight black, but you could just as well use gray, slate blue or even dark green.

After you've completed the layout in pencil, go over your lines with a black marker.

A dark color will help hide an uneven roof.

How to Paint a Colonial-Style Building

4 Alcove and Walls

To create the shadow that gives the illusion of depth, darken the alcove within the pillared entryway. Start with deep gray at the top of the area, then gradually add more white as you work your way down.

Switch to plain white to cover the walls. Try not to paint over your guidelines. Remember to paint all sides of the building.

Shadows add depth to the entryway. Start with dark gray at the top . . .

. . . then gradually add white toward the base.

Paint the walls white, leaving your guidelines showing.

Paint the sides too, and even the back. If you're not sure about windows, you can add them later.

Painting Houses, Cottages and Towns on Rocks

5 Windows

At this point I decided a set of two single windows on each side would leave room for shutters, while more numerous windows might be too small and crowded. I sketched them in first, then filled in the panes with black. I also added windows to either side at this time. Don't forget to paint in the centers of your decorative windows, too.

Pencil in windows on both wings.

Darken the windowpanes with black.

6 Columns

Now fill in the front columns with white, being careful to keep your lines straight and the columns uniform. At the top of each column add a slightly wider oval shape to serve as a capital. When the white is dry, paint a narrow band of deep gray on the left side of each column, creating a shadowed look. If you need to, go over your guidelines with a narrow line of black to ensure the columns stand out crisply from their background. Outline the oval capitals and the front door as well.

Paint the columns carefully with white.

Create shadows on the left side of each column with deep gray.

How to Paint a Colonial-Style Building

7 Facade

Using a small brush and gray paint, create a decorative pattern across the front as shown. If your building is a public one, use this space for lettering.

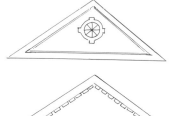

Here are several examples of decorative patterns you can paint on the tympanum.

This is a simple decorative pattern that will dress up the facade.

8 Window and Door Details

I chose deep green for the window shutters. Next I switched to white to detail the windows. Outline the window shape itself, then add lines to indicate the panes. Do the same with the fan window and octagon, too.

To finish the front door, mix a bit of deep gray and subtly indicate a raised panel pattern.

Dark green shutters and delicate white lines bring windows into focus. Add a panel design to the front door.

9 Landscaping

Now all the piece needs is the softening touch of some landscaping. I mixed dark green with a little black to get a very deep shade, and placed squat round boxwoods at the corners and alongside the outside columns. Mix a lighter green to highlight the shrubs and give them fullness. At this point the piece is ready to be displayed, perhaps in your burgeoning rock village.

Neat little bushes add a finishing touch.

Painting Houses, Cottages and Towns on Rocks

More Ideas . . .

If you're steady-handed and would like an even more realistic look, try molding three-dimensional columns with wood filler, as shown in the photos below.

Here's my finished "white house" with a flat front.

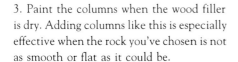

1. To create a three-dimensional look to your columns, carefully squeeze a thick, even line of wood filler over the decorative front just below the roofline.

2. Add another, slightly thinner line below the first, to cover the original guideline. Make a shorter line of wood filler along the base. Squeeze out columns between the base and the top, shaping them one at a time. Use the point of a pencil or the shaft of a paint brush to even up the sides and keep them straight.

3. Paint the columns when the wood filler is dry. Adding columns like this is especially effective when the rock you've chosen is not as smooth or flat as it could be.

Here's an example of a
Southern Colonial, the style
we think of as a "plantation
house."

This is a modified Classic Colonial. The dimensions
have been adjusted to work for a small public library.

This courthouse is similar to the library at left with just a few extra columns
to look "governmental."

This style is true Classic Colonial, sometimes
called Federal. It is the basic style of the
White House and many federal and local
government buildings.

Greek Revival buildings like this one feature columns all around and a more decorative panel above the columns. Some banks or even colleges favor this style.

Here's a Classic Colonial style used for a two-storey home.

These are the rocks shown on the first page of this chapter, now ready to take their respected place in your rock city.

How to Paint a Colonial-Style Building

Painting Houses, Cottages and Towns on Rocks

How to Paint a
Tudor-Style Home

The Tudor-style home, in its many forms, is an impressive structure, featuring massive chimneys, steep roof angles and both dormers and bay windows with diamond-shaped leaded panes. But more than any of these, it is the decorative look of half-timbered siding that sets the Tudor style apart. Inspired by Old English homes, Tudor mansions flourished in America in the twenties and thirties. They regained popularity, though in scaled-down versions, in the seventies, and remain a popular choice in many exclusive neighborhoods.

Due to the "fortress-like" dimensions, this project calls for a more substantial rock. Look for chunky rocks, preferably ones that sit up tall, although there are exceptions (see page 105). Dramatic roof angles are desirable, too. It's also a plus when the roof area has bumps or angles that can be transformed into dormers. If not, you can always add some yourself. Since a gabled end allows for the most decorative half-timbered designs, try to select rocks with triangular facets for that purpose.

Perhaps the easiest way to get a feel for what kind of rock works best is to collect several possible candidates and

What You'll Need

- Acrylic paints in White, Ochre, Black, Brown and Green
- Pencil or pen
- Tube of wood filler

try sketching in some of the features with a pencil. Study the sample rocks below to help determine how you might incorporate some combination of the suggested elements onto each rock. If it doesn't work out one way, scrub off your pencil marks and try another until you come up with a design that is right for the rock.

Many stone shapes will work as Tudor houses, but look for rocks that are taller and have some bumps and angles.

The rock I chose for this project has several features I like. The bottom is nice and flat, the top has the angled look of a steeply pitched roof. Best of all, it has a distinctly triangular side that will be perfect for a decorative gable.

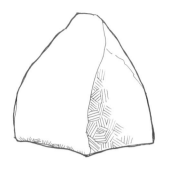

1 Layout

I could have placed the front door in the gabled end, but the composition will be more balanced with the doorway set into the adjoining wall instead. I let the natural shape of the rock suggest where the eaves should go. Once they were established, I divided the gable into two parts. I then divided the first floor in half to indicate where the stonework will start. I carried this horizontal line all the way around.

Next I selected a place at the very top as the site for a chimney. Make the chimney a substantial one, using a generous amount of wood filler.

I also created a square dormer with the wood filler to break up the long sloping angle of the roof. My rock has a funny little knob sticking out on the left side. I decided to turn it into a tree, but could also have made it into a large bay window.

When the wood filler dried, I sketched in the window detail with a marker. Use the ideas on page 107 or examples from magazines to help you choose additional window sites and half-timbered designs that will work on your particular rock. Now the piece is ready for painting.

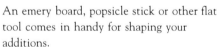

An emery board, popsicle stick or other flat tool comes in handy for shaping your additions.

This bump on the side of my rock can be made into a tree or a bay window.

Here's the final layout, including a wood-filler chimney and dormer.

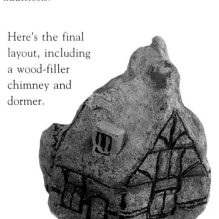
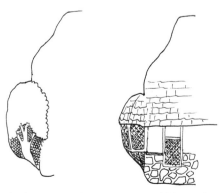

The bump I made into a tree could have also been a bay window.

Painting Houses, Cottages and Towns on Rocks

2 Walls and Windows

Choosing your color scheme might take longer than the actual painting, since there are so many attractive choices. I went with the timeless look of pale gold walls. Add small amounts of Ochre to a puddle of white paint until you reach a shade you like. Use a medium-sized brush to fill in all the wall areas that are not going to be stone or brick. Leave the sketch marks for your half-timbered design showing. Don't forget to paint any dormer fronts and sides.

Next fill in all the windows. You can make them appear lighted-up with yellow, or paint them dark as I did.

3 Stonework Base

For my stonework areas I mixed a deep gray by adding a small amount of white to my black. I covered the entire area that will be set with stones with this color, including the chimney.

Paint the walls, keeping the half-timbered design unpainted for now.

Fill in the window openings.

A deep gray base will set off the stone design later.

Paint the door a warm brown.

Paint the roof with the same warm brown.

4 Cover the Rest of the Rock

For both the front door and the roof I used a medium brown in contrast to all that dark gray. While I had brown on my brush, I also painted a trunk for my tree. I then painted the foliage using a deep forest green. Now all bare portions of the rock are covered.

I'm turning this bump into a dark green tree.

Painting Houses, Cottages and Towns on Rocks

5 Stonework

As always, details give rock houses their appeal. Start by mixing white and black paint to get a light shade of gray. Use a small, short-bristled brush to paint in a mosaic of tiny round stone shapes over the chimney and along the bottom portions of your house. Vary their sizes and shapes, and leave dark spaces showing between them like mortar.

6 Light Details

Switch to a script liner brush to paint narrow eave lines all the way around. Mix a yellow shade lighter than the wall color. Don't worry if you accidently cover up the guidelines between roof and wall since you will want to reemphasize them later anyway.

Use the same yellow color for the diamond-shaped leaded windowpanes. If your window openings are yellow, use dark brown or black instead. First paint a series of diagonal lines in one direction. Then overlap a second set in the opposite direction, creating rows of small diamond-shaped panes.

Fit your stonework together like puzzle pieces both on the chimney and the foundation.

Light-colored eaves help define your rooflines.

Narrow, diagonal crisscrossing lines create diamond-shaped panes.

7 Dark Details

Rinse out your brush and switch to black or deep brown paint. Use this color to redefine the outlines around the doors and windows, between the walls and rockwork, and to fill in the half-timbered designs as shown. Remember to redefine around the dormer window as well.

8 Roof Shingles and Finish

Finally, I used the same white/ochre combination to paint a shingled design over the roof. First, I painted in wiggly horizontal lines, then added vertical shingle lines between them, working from the eaves up to the peak of the roof on both sides. Later I went back and ran a narrow underline of black below each horizontal line to create a shadow effect.

To finish off my tree, I mixed a light yellow and painted a series of ragged, "scribbly" lines of leaves over the deeper green.

Dark outlines define details including your half-timber design.

Add shingles, starting from the bottom of the roof to the top.

A thin dark line under your horizontal shingle lines will add shadows.

Here's my finished Tudor house, complete with tree.

More Ideas . . .

Study the rocks at right and note the wide variety of shapes that will work as a Tudor house. Some shapes need only a wood-filler chimney; others need more extensive additions. Don't pass up a rock that has too many odd angles. It may be perfect for a Tudor!

This is the rock second from left in the group above, all dressed up. Do you see how the wood filler became a tall chimney and a gable?

A very complex design like this would be a fun challenge for more experienced painters.

This is the rock on the front right in the group above. Though Tudors are usually tall, sometimes a wider, shorter rock works.

How to Paint a Tudor-Style Home

More Ideas . . .

Because Tudor-style homes have such a classic look, they are especially attractive as part of a Christmas village. The addition of wreaths, evergreen swags and red bows, plus a snow-covered roof, will transform your Tudor into a seasonal delight. For more dimension, try adding these decorations using the plastic texture paints often used for fabric painting.

This is the same Tudor rock that appears on the previous page. Here I've added pearl white fabric paint on the roof to look like ice, and colored fabric paint for door and window holiday decorations.

Here's an Old English or Shakespearean-style Tudor with a thatched roof.

And here's the same Old English house with a pile of snow on the thatched roof made from pearl white fabric paint, and red and green decorations.

These are the same rocks, finished, that appear on the first page of this chapter with only their layout lines. Do you see how I've taken advantage of odd shapes and angles? Tudor houses can range from small cottages to elegant mansions, but they all have the distinctive features of half-timbered siding, diamond-shaped window panes and steep roof angles.

After you "winterize" your Tudor rock houses, try setting up a charming holiday scene like this.

How to Paint a Tudor-Style Home

Painting Houses, Cottages and Towns on Rocks

How to Paint a
Victorian Mansion

With their timeless elegance and charm, Victorian homes turn as many heads today as they did a century ago. Whether it's the gingerbread trim, the intricate rooflines, towers and turrets or the vibrant color schemes, Victorian-style homes continue to be widely admired, proudly owned and lovingly maintained. Perhaps you can't afford to live in a life-sized "Painted Lady," but you can certainly create your own scaled-down versions on rocks.

There is no hard-and-fast rule as to the best kind of rock to use. Victorian houses range from modest cottages to truly intricate designs that make full use of the facets, knobs and angles of more unusual rocks. Most Victorian rock houses fall somewhere between these extremes.

Hopefully by now you've had plenty of practice at seeing possibilities in the rocks you pick up. Although you should still select rocks with flat bottoms and more or less vertical walls, the best Victorian house rocks offer challenging variations—convoluted sides, strange nooks and crannies, odd angles and knobs that suggest bay windows or towers and other distinctive architecture.

More than any other project in this book, Victorian rocks can be enhanced by the judicious use of wood filler. By extending an eave here, defining a gabled entranceway there, sculpting a turret or adding peaked dormers, you can turn a so-so rock into a real dazzler. The key is to allow the rock's natural contours to guide you in your layout and design.

What You'll Need

- Acrylic paints in Yellow, White, Black, Red and Blue
- Assorted brushes
- Pencil or marker
- Wood filler

I've chosen a rock that offers a number of desirable traits. The peaked roof is well defined and features an attractive gable area and a curved eave on the right side that is interesting and unique. There is also a small notch in the roof above it that would be a perfect place to tuck a decorative window. On the other hand, the left side of the rock is rather featureless, and the area where I envision placing the front door is slightly indented. These flaws can be corrected or concealed with wood filler.

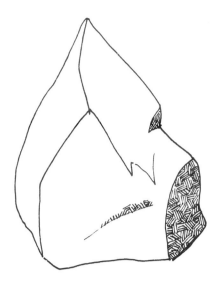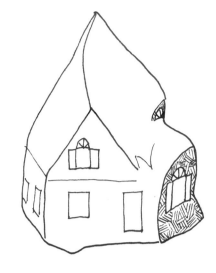

1 Layout

After a thorough scrubbing, use a pencil to sketch in a design using your rock's contours as a guide. When you're satisfied, darken the lines with a marker to make them stand out.

At this point I used wood filler to add an eave to the left side, along with a small dormer window in the roof. In front I continued the eave line around, creating a base for the gable. A second, smaller triangle defines a porch roof above the front door. From it I extended posts down on either side, anchoring them with another short line of wood filler that serves as a front step. The porch posts help hide the slight indentation in the rock's surface behind them. Finally, I perched a delicate chimney on the side of the roof. Allow any wood-filler additions to dry and harden thoroughly before going on.

Add eaves and a dormer with wood filler.

Forming an entryway around the front door adds interest.

2 Color Scheme

While deciding on a color scheme, I went through my photo collection of "Painted Ladies." After sketching out the house's basic design on paper, I experimented with several different color combinations. I settled on a cheerful mix of sunny yellow, peach and white, with a gray roof.

First I mixed lemon yellow and white to reach the pale pastel yellow shade I wanted. With a medium-sized brush, I colored in the walls all the way around, leaving a narrow foundation unpainted at the bottom. Don't forget to paint the sides of any dormer windows and other features, such as the half-round window tucked into the roof. Switch to a narrow brush for hard-to-reach places in corners and around the posts.

3 Shadows

Next I mixed a touch of black into my pastel yellow to get a yellowish-gray and used it to paint a strip of shadow below the eaves. Under the porch roof I wanted even more shadow and extended the gray nearly halfway down on both sides of the door.

Paint the walls, but leave the foundation unpainted.

Shadows under the eaves add depth and realism.

Add a more shaded area below the porch roof.

4 Roof and Windows

To paint the roof I mixed black and white, heavier on the white, for a paler gray. I applied it with my large brush for quick coverage, switching to a smaller brush to paint around the wood-filler additions.

Use black to fill in window openings, including dormers and half-round windows. My rock is some kind of shale, and fairly dark to begin with, but darkening the windows adds definition. Paint the foundation around the base black as well.

Cover the roof, switching to a small brush around tricky areas.

Outline the dormer windows with the wall color, then darken all the window openings.

Painting Houses, Cottages and Towns on Rocks

5 Gables

To mix peach for the gables, I started with the same pastel yellow that was used for the walls. Next to it I mixed a drop of red with a drop of white to make deep pink. I added this pink to my yellow in tiny increments until I reached just the right shade of pastel peach.

Peach gables lend cheery contrast. Carefully outline the window area in the large gable.

6 Chimney and Door

Now the only uncovered portions are the chimney, front door and porch. For the chimney I used the deep pink left over from mixing my peach paint and added a brushtip's worth of black to get a reddish-brown color suggestive of brick.

Then I added a touch more black to dull the reddish tone further and painted the door with this color.

Paint the chimney a brick-like color.

Paint the door a wood color.

7 White Trim

Crisp white trim will really pull this color scheme together. Often on Victorian houses, the trim is a darker or lighter shade of the wall color, or another color altogether. Experiment with a variety of colors for your house, or stick with white as I've done here.

Starting with the eaves, paint a strip of white over the gray roof along the edges. Where you have wood-filler overhangs, make sure the bottom sides are painted, too.

Taking care to keep the trim narrow and even, outline the slanting sides of the large gable and all around the porch, including the posts, landing and step.

Don't forget your special rooflines.

Use a script liner brush to paint a narrow white line of trim at the corners of the house. Extend these corner lines all the way to the base of the rock.

Outline around the windows with the script liner, too.

Painting Houses, Cottages and Towns on Rocks

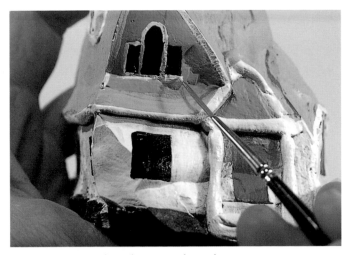

Take your time to keep lines straight and even.

Also outline around the door at this time.

An oval glass set into the front door will dress it up. Use black paint and a small brush to darken the oval.

As I was preparing to outline the front windows I noticed that my lower window was not aligned with the window in the gable above. To correct the problem I added a strip of black to one side of the lower window, then mixed up a little pale yellow and covered the edge on the other side, effectively shifting the window into better alignment. After the paint dried, I went on to outline it with white.

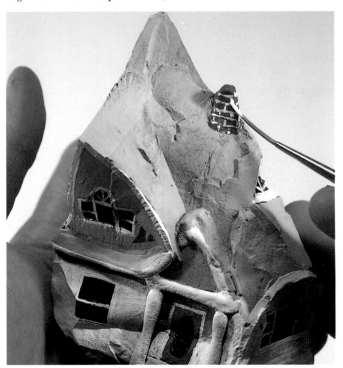

To detail the chimney, add several horizontal brick lines, then break them up with staggered vertical lines.

8 Scalloped Shingles

Rows of scalloped shingles are the perfect touch to finish a Victorian roof. Mix a gray darker than the roof. Begin with the plainest side, and work up from the bottom, using the tip of a script liner to form a line of connected *U* shapes. At the next row start with half a *U* so that each subsequent shingle will be centered on the upright line of the shingle below. On dormer roofs change direction to follow the smaller roofline.

If your roof has complex angles, as mine does on the right side, you may want to pencil in some guidelines to keep your rows looking straight. Always start at the bottom and work up, following the outside edges of the roof. If you need to change direction or adjust shingle spacing, do it in the center where it won't be so noticeable. Remember, you can always repaint your roof and try again if your first attempt looks too crooked.

Rows of *U*-shaped shingles create a scalloped pattern.

Keep the shingles straight and even along the eaves but change direction to go with your varied roof lines.

Painting Houses, Cottages and Towns on Rocks

9 Latticework

To finish the dark foundation area around the base with latticework, paint a series of white slanting lines all the way around, then go back and cross them with a stroke slanting in the opposite direction.

For the lattice trim start with diagonal strokes in one direction.

Go back and do diagonal strokes in the opposite direction.

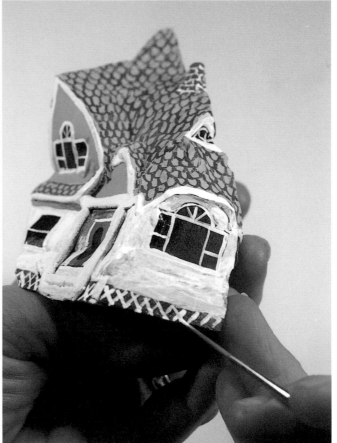

Paint latticework on all sides of the foundation.

How to Paint a Victorian Mansion

10 Gable Detail

You may choose to leave the peach gables plain, line them with vertical or horizontal lapped siding, or cover them with a scallop pattern. For something different, I tried a diamond shingle pattern. I mixed red, white and a bit of black to get the same brick color I used on the chimney, and used the tip of my script liner to make a series of fine diagonal lines across the gable. Then, turning the rock to keep the lines straight, I painted a second set of diagonal lines crisscrossing the first to create a series of small diamonds.

First paint very fine diagonal lines across the gable.

Crisscrossing diagonals create a diamond pattern. Turn your rock whatever way is most comfortable.

Leave a small space around the windows, and then outline around the windows with the same color.

Paint the smaller gable the same way.

Painting Houses, Cottages and Towns on Rocks

11 Siding

To detail the yellow walls, I mixed up a small amount of the same yellowish-gray I used earlier for shadowing. I carefully indicated rows of clapboard siding, allowing my brush to skip here and there to keep the lines light and rather indistinct. I carried the lines into the lower portion of the porch and around the house on both sides. Then I added a brushful of white to the yellow-gray mix to lighten it, and added some siding lines to the shadowy area around and above the door.

Narrow lines suggest clapboard siding.

Use paler lines to show up against the shadowed entryway.

12 Finishing Touches
All that's left is to add trim and accentuate the details.

Use a deep gray and a script liner to outline around the white trim of the windows and door. Either outline the windows all the way around, or just on one side and along the bottom, as I did here, to make the light appear to be coming from one side.

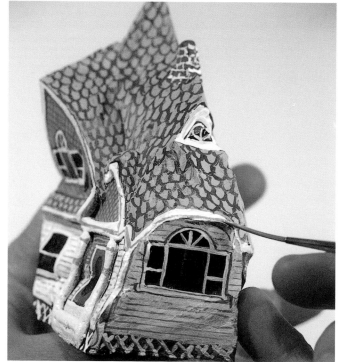

I decided to add narrow bands of peach trim along the eaves and on the upper porch posts for even more decorative interest.

Painting Houses, Cottages and Towns on Rocks

To define the steps, use dark gray to outline the steps and the landing.

For a more lived-in look, use white paint and the very tip of your script liner to stipple in a suggestion of lace curtains in the windows.

Finally, add a touch of blue to the white and stroke a couple of diagonal "streaks" across the window and door glass. All that's left is to sign it on the bottom, then spray it with clear acrylic finish to protect the paint.

121

More Ideas . . .

Victorian houses make wonderful accent pieces or gifts. There are so many variations that it's hard to imagine ever getting tired of painting them.

This is a great find for a Victorian rock house.

Here's how I fixed it up with wood filler and laid out the design.

This pink house is a fairly simple Victorian design. At left from top to bottom is the plain rock, the wood-filler additions (note the turret on the left side!), and the pencilled-in design.

Here is a complex house with many wings and front pillars. I used two green colors on the roof for added depth.

You might try a "haunted house," complete with ghostly inhabitants.

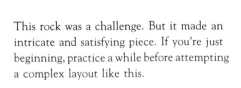

This rock was a challenge. But it made an intricate and satisfying piece. If you're just beginning, practice a while before attempting a complex layout like this.

How to Paint a Victorian Mansion

Create Your Own Rock Villages

Once you've accumulated a number of rock cottages, buildings and shops, try arranging them in a village setting. You can dream up your own setting, or even replicate an area of your hometown.

Create a realistic backdrop for your village, either inside or out on your porch or in your garden. Indoors, try using a scrap of green carpet, Astroturf or terry cloth squares molded over shaped Styrofoam, or folded fabric hills. Paint your own trees and shrubs on rocks, or buy landscaping elements used by model train hobbyists.

Outside, cover dirt or peat moss hills with bits of moss and sedge. To make roads, use kitty litter "gravel," sand or roofing shingles cut into curving lanes with heavy duty scissors. Saw-dust and dried weeds and flowers all make attractive landscaping elements.

Create Your Own Rock Villages

Painting Houses, Cottages and Towns on Rocks

Index